Thomas Brändle

Selection of Public Servants into Politics

An Economic Analysis of Its Causes and Consequences

Nomos

Die Deutsche Nationalbibliothek verzeichnet diese Publikation in der Deutschen Nationalbibliografie; detaillierte bibliografische Daten sind im Internet über http://dnb.d-nb.de abrufbar.

Die Deutsche Nationalbibliothek lists this publication in the Deutsche Nationalbibliografie; detailed bibliographic data is available in the Internet at http://dnb.d-nb.de .

Zugl.: Basel, Universität, Diss., 2012

ISBN 978-3-8487-0307-4

1. Auflage 2013

Preface

Traditional political economy considers good government mainly the result of properly designed institutions that shape the incentives of those who make policy. However, good government is not only a matter of incentives but also of selection. Accordingly, two questions define a major challenge and attract a great deal of attention in current political economy: How does the selection of politicians with different identity and quality characteristics influence policy choice? And, what determines the selection of heterogeneous politicians in the first place? In this book, which is a doctoral thesis written and available at the University of Basel, I select one important quality dimension; i.e., the professional background of politicians. In particular, I concentrate on the selection of public servants into politics and want to better understand its causes and consequences.

The primary research interest was motivated by circumstantial evidence showing that public servants are strongly represented in many parliaments of Western democracies. Due to current policy debates in Switzerland and Germany, I became aware of substantial institutional differences among jurisdictions regarding the rules which govern the (in)compatibility of a public service position with a legislative mandate. Thus, the first major research question to be addressed was: Do differences in these rules systematically affect the incentives to run for political office for candidates with a public sector background? Subsequently, I wanted to gain a better understanding of the consequences for political processes and outcomes. Of particular interest was whether differences in the representation of public servants in parliament impact legislative oversight processes, and whether these differences help to explain corruption and public sector growth. The results of the present book indicate that institutions, primarily set up to hold politicians accountable, systematically influence the composition of the pool of politicians and affect political outcomes also via the channel of selection.

The research on public servants in politics has been an intellectual stimulation and a challenge. First of all, I could contribute to the flourishing literature on the selection of politicians being a new and complementary line of research in political economy. Second, the topic itself and closely related questions have frequently provoked innovative and critical conversations which challenged traditional political economy. Furthermore, gaining a deeper knowledge of political institutions and the strict economic analysis of the resulting incentives for the selection and the behavior of political agents were highly interesting and scientifically fruitful activities. The acquainted knowledge on and the broader economic understanding of a wide range of political institutions will constitute the basis for future research.

The main chapters (chapters III to VI) analyze different aspects of the selection of public servants into politics. All main chapters can be read as stand alone contributions. Different or earlier versions of these chapters have all been presented at national and international conferences, workshops and research seminars on invitation. These conferences and workshops include, among others, the Annual Meetings of the European Public Choice Society in Athens and Rennes, the Annual Meeting of the German Economic Association (*Verein für Socialpolitik*) in Frankfurt, the Annual Meetings of the Swiss Society of Economics and Statistics in Geneva, Fribourg, Lucerne and Zürich, and the 18th Silvaplana Workshop in Political Economy. Presentations on invitation were given in the research seminar at Bocconi University, Milan, the University of Siena, the Max-Planck-Institute for Research on Collective Goods, Bonn, in 2010, the University of Lugano in 2011, and at the University of Mannheim in 2012.

I am deeply indebted to my Ph.D. advisor and mentor Professor Dr. Alois Stutzer. His guidance and continuing support as well as his openness to discuss research ideas and projects have been an extraordinary experience. Working under his supervision and in collaboration with him fundamentally strengthened my economic skills, particularly my analytical rigor, and introduced me to research. I consider this period a privilege and I am looking forward to continuing our research projects. I would also like to thank my second advisor Professor Dr. Dr. h.c. mult. Bruno S. Frey for his support and the valuable feedback. The meetings with him were a great source of inspiration.

I would like to express my gratitude to Professor Dr. Vincenzo Galasso and Professor Dr. Tommaso Nannicini for inviting me to the Ettore Bocconi Department of Economics and IGIER at Bocconi University, Milan in 2010. I greatly benefited from their feedback and the time spent in this outstanding scientific environment. Related to this, I would like to thank the Basel private bankers for sponsoring the award for young scientists making this leave of absence for research possible. Moreover, I owe thanks to Professor Dr. Mario Jametti for inviting me to the Institute for Microeconomics and Public Economics at the University of Lugano and to Professor Dr. Maurizio Cotta for the invitation to the Center for the Study of Political Change (CIRCaP) at the University of Siena. All of these research stays were excellent opportunities to present, discuss and improve my research as well as to get into contact with often different but complementary perspectives on political economy. In addition, I would like to thank Professor Dr. Silvio Borner, Dr. Pierre Boyer, Professor Dr. Alessandra Casarico, Professor Dr. Reiner Eichenberger, Dr. Michael Funk, Professor Dr. Simon Luechinger, Professor Dr. Mark Schelker, and Dr. David Stadelmann for the very interesting conversations and the constructive criticism.

For the many suggestions, the in-depth discussions and the proofreading of single chapters, my special thanks go to Thorsten Henne, Alexander Maier, Ulrich Matter, Dr. Manuela Merki, Reto Odermatt, Arvid Schors, Michael Zehnder and Anna Zeiser.

Moreover, I am grateful for the financial support by the Basler Studienstiftung for the production of the book.

Last but not least, I would like to thank my father. I deeply appreciate his unconditional support from the very beginning.

Basel, April 2012 Thomas Brändle

Contents

List of Figures

List of Tables

Chapter I: Introduction

Traditional political economy considers good government primarily the result of properly designed institutions that shape the incentives of those who make policy. However, good government is not only a matter of incentives but also of selection. Accordingly, two questions define a major challenge and attract a great deal of attention in current political economy: How does the selection of politicians with different identity and quality characteristics influence policy choice? And, what determines the selection of heterogeneous politicians in the first place? We select one important quality dimension; i.e., the professional background of politicians. It fundamentally shapes the personal socio-economic conditions influencing an individual's decision to run for office and it shapes private economic interests once elected. In particular, we concentrate on the selection of public servants into politics.[1]

The analysis of public servants in politics is of high interest and relevance for at least three reasons. First, public servants form a large professional group present in most national legislatures. This disproportionality in representation with respect to professional background sparks concerns regarding descriptive representation as (work) life experiences of the representatives differ systematically from those of the represented.[2] Second and more importantly, personal unions and affiliations between the legislature and the public service as well as the perk of guaranteed reemployment compromise the constitutionally proposed political neutrality of the public service and, in more general terms, undermine the separation of powers. The double role as agents in public service and as principals who supervise the public service in parliament generates a conflict of interest. Persons holding both a legislative and an executive position may face decisions as legislators that affect their role in the executive branch, for instance, when voting on the proper department's budget. In contrast to all other members of parliament, we consider this conflict of interest as immanent as it involves a sovereign area of government activity. However, public servants also form a pool of people with first-hand information about public service issues and a revealed interest in these matters. Thus, electing insiders to parliament who become accountable to the electorate can serve as a source of expertise and even as a check in the legislative process. Third, due to concerns about the conflicts of interest and the politicization of the public service, in many countries, public servants pursuing a political office are subject to special legislation. These con-

1 In this group, we include all employees that concurrently hold public law work contracts and receive public sector pay. Public servants elected to parliament generally come from professions in education (i.e., teachers or university professors), various fields of public administration, the judiciary, the police, and the armed forces.

2 Professional background is one dimension of descriptive representation following the categorization of Pitkin (1967). The concept of descriptive political representation is central in political science. We do, however, not further discuss the selection of public servants into politics from a descriptive representation perspective.

stitutional provisions either specify the incompatibility of a public sector position with a legislative mandate or even declare public servants ineligible for candidacy.

The present book mainly pursues the objective to investigate the institutional determinants and the consequences of the selection of public servants into politics. In particular, we want to analyze whether incompatibility rules, traditionally considered as (ex-ante) sanctioning instruments, and a broader set of related institutions have an effect on the decision to enter politics. Subsequently, we want to gain a better understanding of the consequences for political outcomes such as corruption or public sector growth, which might also accrue from differences in the representation of public servants in politics. Integrating both research questions, we want to better understand institutions not only as to how they reduce conflicts of interest and increase political accountability but also as to how they alter the incentives to enter politics and thus affect political outcomes via the channel of selection.

The research questions are analyzed from a political economics perspective.[3] For each analysis, a theoretical framework is set up from which hypotheses are derived. Thereby, we mainly concentrate on the supply of politicians.[4] The hypotheses are empirically tested once in a cross-country setting to provide first macro-evidence and three times in more detail within the institutional framework of the German Laender (as the federal states are called). We study German Laender parliaments mainly for two reasons. First, legislators with a public service occupational background are a striking feature of German politics (see Chapters III and IV). Second, German Laender have legislative competencies in public education, public security, and public administration, which includes the ministerial bureaucracy in terms of budget and personnel (see Chapter VI). In addition, a central mandate of the German Laender parliaments is oversight (see Chapter V). The empirical investigations required, in particular, the extensive and careful collection of the fraction of public servants elected to parliament and the specific institutional provisions in force in the respective jurisdictions.

Our contribution to research can be stated as follows. First, we add to the emerging and prominent literature on political selection by highlighting one important quality dimension of politicians; i.e., professional background. We focus on public servants and show this group to be, on average, the single largest professional group present in national legislatures. Second, evidence is offered supporting that i) institutions impact political selection and ii) the identity of politicians in terms of their professional background matters for political processes and outcomes. Third, we analyze the so far neglected institution of incompatibility - though being one fundamental facet of the separation of powers - and introduce it to political economics research. Thereby, the complementary view of political institutions in providing both, selection and sanc-

3 Throughout the book the terms 'political economy' and 'political economics' are used interchangeably. The emphasis is clearly on the economic approach to the study of politics. We are, however, aware that the term 'political economy' is traditionally used to describe a much broader field subsuming, among others, monetary, fiscal, international, political, public and health economics.

4 We assume the selection into politics to be supply-dominated (see Besley 2005 as well as Norris and Lovenduski 1993 for a similar reasoning). The demand for politicians is addressed when we discuss the role of parties under alternative electoral rules in Chapter II and public servants as voters in Chapter IV.

tioning devices is underlined. The insights provide an improved understanding of the mechanisms inducing policy outcomes - whether these outcomes - are more the result of political selection or of holding politicians accountable, or whether both mechanisms systematically interact. Finally, the insights broaden the basis for considerations about the constitutional design of political institutions in general and the personal separation of powers regarding public servants in parliament in particular.

Chapter II gives an introduction into the economics of political selection. Chapters III to VI focus solely on the selection of public servants into politics and include empirical analyses. Chapter VII concludes.

We start in chapter II with briefly presenting the traditional political economy perspective which has paid primary attention to the structuring of the principal-agent relationship between citizens and politicians and the role of competition in disciplining political agents. Then, we give reasons for the complementary approach which emphasizes that good government is also the result of selecting sound political agents. In the next step, we want to gain a better understanding of the institutional conditions which influence the selection of people with different quality characteristics into politics. We discuss important recent contributions which study the selection effects of the compensation of politicians and of parties under alternative electoral rules. We then focus on professional background and discuss the selection of two prominent professional groups into politics; i.e., businessmen and lawyers. Thereby, particular attention will be paid to the underlying institutional structure. We conclude with a short discussion pointing to questions of further interest and relevance.

In chapter III, we document the phenomenon of the strong representation of public servants in national legislatures. We present a newly compiled data set on the professional composition of the first parliamentary chamber in 71 countries for the years 2000 to 2010. We proceed with the analysis of the determinants of the variation in the representation of public servants in politics. In particular, we study constitutional provisions that primarily aim to inhibit conflicts of interest; i.e., the different regimes that define the (in)compatibility of public service employment with a legislative mandate. Accordingly, data is collected on the (in)compatibility regimes for the same 71 countries. It is hypothesized that the stricter the incompatibility provisions are, the less attractive is a political mandate for public servants. Moreover, an initial basis is provided to explore the consequences that a strong representation of public servants in national parliaments has for the political process and political outcomes. We examine the relationship between the political selection of public servants and corruption as well as the size of the government sector.

In the next chapter, we rivet on the determinants of the selection of public servants into politics in more detail. We develop a general political economics framework to study a public servant's incentives to pursue a candidacy for a parliamentary mandate. The theoretical focus is on issues of incompatibility and a wide set of related institutions that determine, in a comparative perspective, the cost-benefit calculus of running for a seat in parliament. We investigate, for example, the compensation for holding office in abeyance during parliamentary membership, subsequent automatic promotion and special pension benefits. The theoretical considerations are expanded with a short discussion of the role of public servants as voters. We refer to the institutional framework of the German Laender to substantiate the theoretical arguments with empirical evidence.

In chapter V, we turn to the analysis of legislative processes. We concentrate on parliamentary oversight as one fundamental legislative mandate and important instrument to control and influence the executive branch's efficient provision of public goods and services. We propose a framework which incorporates the identity of legislators into a political economics analysis of parliamentary oversight. Legislators decide about the effort they invest in oversight depending on their individual control costs and the level of electoral competition. Public servants elected to parliament face a conflict of interest but also have lower control costs due to their experience and information advantage. If held accountable, oversight becomes a relatively attractive activity for them to win votes. We present empirical evidence on the use of parliamentary control instruments for the German Laender.

Chapter VI studies the growth of senior official employment in the ministerial bureaucracy. Senior ministerial officials are entrusted with the operational governance of the public service and their number has grown enormously since World War II. We argue that the selection of public servants into politics is of particular interest for better understanding growth in senior official employment. The professional interests of public servants elected to parliament might systematically bias legislative outcomes in favor of inflated ministerial employment as there exist close personal linkages or personal unions between the legislature (and in particular public servants elected to the legislature) and high-ranking ministerial bureaucrats. We refer to senior official employment in the ministerial bureaucracies of the German Laender to provide empirical evidence.

In the last chapter, we summarize the essential results of each contribution. We discuss the implications for economic advice on the constitutional stage and conclude with implications for economic research.

Chapter II: Economics of Political Selection

This chapter provides an introduction to the evolving research on political selection. In Section 1, the importance of taking into account the complementary roles of sanctioning and selection for the economic analysis of politics is emphasized. In Section 2, we want to gain a better understanding of the institutions that systematically affect the selection of politicians. In particular, we take a closer look at the pay for politicians and the role of parties under alternative electoral rules. In preparation of the main topic of the book, we turn in Section 3 to the political selection of people with different professional backgrounds. Two prominent groups; i.e., businessmen and lawyers are selected. We ask which institutional conditions influence the attractiveness of a political mandate for these two groups. Section 4 concludes with a short discussion in which a variety of further research questions will be pointed out.

1 Two complementary views: sanctioning and selection

1.1 Political sanctioning

In order to achieve good government, research in political economy has addressed the major concern of how to induce political agents to act in the interest of their principals. Put differently, how to accomplish discipline and accountability of the decision-makers. Most attention has been paid to the structuring of the principal-agent relationship between citizens and politicians and the appropriate design of political institutions. In particular, elections and the corresponding design of the electoral system are considered the major means to provide the proper incentives to politicians (see Besley 2005 and Besley 2006 for this reasoning).

Similar to the market for goods and services, an electoral system which is aimed at enhancing competition among politicians should result in policy choices which are closer to citizens' preferences. (Re-)electoral incentives and thus the competition for votes discipline the political agents once in the formation of their policy platforms (pre-electoral competition) and once in the behavior in office (post-electoral competition). The motivation of political agents is traditionally modeled as being opportunistic including office and rent-seeking, and as being partisan.

In models of pre-electoral competition, electoral promises are considered binding and enforceable.[1] The candidates adjust their policy platforms in order to maximize their chances of winning elections. Once elected, the political agent implements his announced policy. The formation of the policy platform is central to the choice of policy. Elections function to select policies which are dominated by the preferences of the median voter. The more competitive elections are, the stronger is the incentive for candidates to adopt a "middle ground policy platform" to please voters. In models of

1 Basic models of pre-electoral competition have further restrictive assumptions, such as an unidimensional policy space, single-peaked preferences and a two-party competition.

pre-electoral competition without partisan considerations, the selection of candidates with heterogeneous quality characteristics does not matter at all. Disciplining the formation of policy platforms is described in models following Downs (1957).[2]

In models of post-electoral competition, electoral promises are considered as non-binding. Politicians are elected without a clear and enforceable mandate and political constitutions are considered incomplete contracts. Rather than selecting policies, elections serve to select politicians based on their ideology and most importantly on their past behavior (in office). Disciplining the politicians while in office is achieved if there are re-electoral incentives and voters who vote retrospectively. Post-electoral politics is analyzed in political agency models following the tradition of Barro (1973) and Ferejohn (1986).

In both, pre-electoral and post-electoral approaches to the analysis of electoral competition, politicians and voters are separate entities and the existence of the former group is exogenously given. Moreover, in each class of models politicians are assumed to be a homogeneous group. The selection process and the identity of politicians do not matter.[3]

On the basis of both analytical frameworks, further institutions are analyzed as to how they shape the incentives for behavior and structure political competition. This can be briefly illustrated when comparing a majoritarian electoral system to a proportional electoral system, and a more to a less independent media system. For example, in pre-electoral politics, a majoritarian electoral system and an independent media system make the commitment and the positioning of candidates within the policy space easier. In post-electoral politics, majority voting and more transparency in politics through independent media facilitate the control of politicians and thus the electoral sanctioning of politicians since policy choices are better individually attributable. The importance of and the relative attention paid to the design of political institutions compared to considerations regarding selection is, for instance, explicitly stated by Buchanan (1989, p.18) who argues that: "[To] improve politics, it is necessary to improve or reform rules. There is no suggestion that improvement lies in the selection of morally superior agents who will use their powers in some public interest."

1.2 Political selection

This traditional perspective on competitive elections (within a properly designed electoral system) as disciplining devices has, however, recently been challenged. The complementary perspective places emphasis on elections as devices to select politicians with different identity and quality characteristics.

2 In models of pre-electoral competition, partisan considerations are introduced with the help of probabilistic voting models. When choosing the policy platforms, the candidates make a trade-off between their partisan policy preferences and their desire to win the election. In contrast to the median voter model, in which policy convergence is the result of (strong) electoral competition, complete policy divergence can occur in models with partisan loyalties. The partisan motivation is pioneered by Wittman (1977, 1983) and Alesina (1988).

3 Standard models of post-electoral competition focus on moral hazard problems. However, extensions also include adverse selection. For example, Besley and Case (1995) and Fearon (1999) model different types of politicians with respect to motivation. For a discussion of political agency models see Besley (2006).

Firstly, every political process in representative or (semi-)direct democracies inherently comprises the delegation of decision-making power to elected representatives for uncertain future circumstances. One might expect that decisions are taken differently depending on the individual competence and background of the representatives. Secondly, the degree to which politicians can credibly commit to policy platforms is limited. Nonbinding electoral promises suggest that the selection of political agents who credibly represent and implement a certain policy is of crucial importance. Thirdly, the instruments available for controlling politicians through elections and other institutional provisions are limited. The (ab-)use of the resulting discretion in office thus depends on the quality of the politicians (see Besley 2005).

The complementary perspective comes along with a new approach to study politicians. The focus is shifted towards the challenging question of who decides to become a politician. The (self-)selection into politics is thus modeled as endogenous. Osborne and Slivinsky (1996) and Besley and Coate (1997) are the first contributions to present the so-called citizen-candidate framework. In this alternative approach to the Downsian model, the artificial distinction between citizens and political agents is lifted as the politicians are selected by the citizens from the citizens who decide to enter the political market in the first place. The decision to enter politics depends on the individual costs and benefits accruing to the political office. Electoral promises become credible because appropriate candidates are found in the electoral process. Once elected, the politician implements his most preferred policy.[4]

Obviously, the selection of high-quality candidates is desirable and becomes a major concern. In the recent theoretical literature (see below), political quality is considered as the ability of politicians to provide public goods at low cost. Besley (2005) argues that political quality comprises essentially two aspects; i.e., competence and honesty. With ease, these two dimensions of quality characteristics can be further disaggregated. Political competence involves (certain) leadership and persuasion skills, and the ability to understand and analyze politics. These skills might be innate or acquired during education, professional life and previous political engagement. The same (background) indicators; i.e., the level and choice of education, the previous professional and political experience signal quality to citizens. Regarding honesty in politics, one might think of characteristics such as trustworthiness, integrity and loyalty or the related idea that politicians should have a public service motivation (see Besley 2005).[5] Evidently, this

4 Osborne and Slivinski (1996) as well as Besely and Coate (1997) model politics as a three-stage process. In the first stage, the focus is on what determines a candidate's entry decision. In the second stage, citizens decide for whom to vote for. In the last stage, the candidates who have won implement their most preferred policies. The major innovation is the first stage introducing an endogenous supply of politicians. See also Serna (1995) for an excellent and very early discussion of the supply and demand-side considerations in the market for politicians from a public choice perspective. A related model of political recruitment taking into account supply and demand-side considerations is presented by the political scientists Norris and Lovenduski (1995). For related ideas on political selection see Fearon (1999), Patzelt (1999) and Mansbridge (2009).

5 Since there is no agreed model of honesty, Besley (2006) proposes a model of fiduciary duty to approach honesty in politics. Closely related considerations, such as the concept of civic virtue and the role of moral dispositions in politics are discussed in Brennan and Hamlin (2000).

concept of political quality is simplified, concentrates on ex-ante quality and is far from conclusive as research is evolving.

In fact, important recent research shows that the identity of politicians matters for political outcomes. Jones and Olken (2005) find that unexpected deaths of national leaders influence economic growth. This is the more the case, the more the political systems lean towards autocracy. Besley et al. (2011) offer evidence that the education of national leaders positively affects economic performance.[6] Chattopadhyay and Duflo (2004) study the impact of political reservation for women in India on local public goods provision. They find that political decision makers invest more in public goods relevant to the demand of their own genders. For India, Pande (2003) studies political reservation for politically disadvantaged groups. She finds that political reservation for scheduled castes and tribes increases the redistribution of resources in favor of the groups that benefit from political reservation.

If the composition of the pool of politicians impacts political outcomes, then, indeed a better understanding of how politicians are selected is essential. In particular, the question arises as to whether institutional conditions can be identified that systematically affect the attractiveness of a political office for candidates of different quality.

2 Which institutions impact political selection?

A crucial issue in the comparative institutional analysis of political selection is whether the regime type matters. One might expect different compositions of the pool of politicians depending on the type and the degree of democracy. On the one extreme, there might be systematically different incentives to enter politics in a (semi-)direct democracy (compared to a representative democracy) where politicians are much more subject to citizens' control. On the other extreme, the pool of politicians in more autocratic systems seems to be dominated by low-quality politicians who abuse their office for self-dealing. One first piece of evidence is presented by Besley and Reynal-Querol (2011). They approximate heterogeneity in the competence of politicians with the formal level of education. In their extensive empirical investigation, better educated politicians are observed more frequently as leaders in democracies than in autocracies. Another unexplored question is whether different levels of government with differences in the sovereign authority assigned to each level of government attract different candidates.[7] Moreover, institutions generating transparency in the political market might affect who decides to become a politician. One can think of selection effects due to higher scrutiny of politicians' behavior induced by independent media and – consid-

6 In the related field of corporate governance, recent analyses of corporate performance emphasize the significance of the identity of the chief executive officers (CEOs). For an example, see Bertrand and Schoar (2003). Another prominent area, where selection with regards to quality characteristics is widely accepted is the monetary policy literature.

7 A related question is whether elections on different levels of government serve as (quality) filters. For a first contribution, see Cooter (2002).

ered more narrowly or in addition – by stricter disclosure rules for politicians.[8] Further institutional features that vary across jurisdictions and are likely to be relevant to an improved understanding of political selection include the remuneration of politicians, parties, electoral rules, primaries, (gender) quotas, term limits, incompatibility rules, and even immunity rules.[9] Many of these institutions have been analyzed by political economists regarding their capacity to generate political accountability. However, the complementary view of these institutions in providing incentives for selection has received much less attention.

2.1 Pay for politicians

In this section, we focus on pay for politicians as an important institutional determinant of the decision to enter politics. In addition, we open up the perspective and briefly discuss further monetary returns to political office; i.e., outside and post-office earnings which might affect the attractiveness of entering politics.

Following the traditional perspective in political economics, the effect of salaries on a politician's discipline and his performance, respectively have been analyzed in political agency models.[10]

How changes in salaries influence the incentive to run for political office has just recently been addressed by political economists. According to Besley (2005), the attractiveness of holding political offices mainly stems from three sources: pay, public service motivation and extractable rents.[11] Low-quality politicians ("bad politicians") are motivated by pay and extractable rents. High-quality politicians ("good politicians") care about pay and public service motivation. In order to think about how various aspects change the composition of the pool of candidates and politicians, Besley (2005) proposes an attractiveness ratio defined as (rents + wages)/(public service motivation + wages). The smaller the attractiveness ratio is the more high-quality candidates will enter politics. In this framework, the effect of an increase in pay on the selection of high-quality politicians ("good politicians") depends on the relative strength of rents and public service motivation in attracting candidates. If public service motivation is more important than rents for many citizens, an increase in pay leads to a lower average quality of politicians. If rents are more relevant than public service motivation for many citizens, then,

8 As to disclosure in politics, Djankov et al. (2010) present a unique data set on the de jure and de facto disclosure by politicians for far more than 100 countries inviting further comparative analyses regarding accountability and selection in politics.

9 See Dal Bó et al. (2006) for an excellent theoretical discussion of how threat and violence can affect self-selection into politics and how the existence of immunity rules positively impacts the cost-benefit calculus of running for political office.

10 For example, Besley (2004) shows that, given the possibility of re-election, as the value of office holding increases, politicians are more likely to abstain from rent-seeking activities and behave more in congruence with citizens' preferences. He also presents empirical evidence supporting the positive incentive effect of a higher salary. This reasoning is closely related to the efficiency-wage theory in labor economics following the contributions by Akerlof (1982) and Shapiro and Stiglitz (1984).

11 Politicians with a public service motivation can be understood as agents who derive more utility from serving in political office than other politicians. They are intrinsically motivated to serve the public interest and enjoy carrying out their task (Frey 1997).

an increase in pay leads to a situation in which holding a political office becomes more attractive to high-quality candidates.

Caselli and Morelli (2004) present a citizen candidate model where low-quality politicians ("bad politicians") have a comparative advantage in holding political office. A positive relation between political competence and competence in the private market is assumed. Accordingly, the opportunity costs of low-quality candidates are lower than those of the high-quality candidates since they face worse opportunities in the private sector. One central result is that higher relative pay increases the average quality of politicians, as candidates with higher opportunity costs (self-)select into politics.[12]

In the same analytical framework, Messner and Pohlborn (2004) come to a different comparative static result. The direct selection effect is also positive; i.e., a higher salary renders the political office more attractive to candidates of high quality. However, as long as the political office is relatively unattractive and not well paid there is also an indirect effect of an increase in pay; i.e., all other candidates (of lower quality) have more incentives to run. A higher probability that candidates of low-quality run makes it more attractive for the candidate of high quality to free ride on low-quality candidates by not running for political office. Only for sufficiently high levels of pay does the political office become more attractive and eventually the direct selection effect dominates.

Mattozzi and Merlo (2008) show in a dynamic equilibrium overlapping generations model of the career of politicians that an increase in the salary paid to politicians has different selection effects on either "career politicians" (politicians until retirement) or individuals with "political careers" (politicians who stay in politics only for a while to signal their quality to the private sector). An increase in pay in the political market renders this market more attractive to candidates of all quality levels. This lowers the quality of the worst citizen who becomes a politician (entry effect). Since the political pay has become more attractive, high-quality incumbent politicians have, however, a stronger incentive to remain in politics (retention effect). The effect on the average quality of individuals with "political careers" is negative. The effect on the average quality of "career politicians" is ambiguous and depends on the relative strength of the retention and the entry effect.

Shifting the focus towards empirical contributions, Ferraz and Finan (2009) analyze an exogenous variation in the pay of local politicians across Brazilian municipalities for elections held in 2000 and 2004. They address the potential endogeneity concern of politicians' pay being set by the politicians themselves by exploiting a constitutional amendment. The amendment introduced a cap depending on the municipality's pop-

12 The prediction of Caselli and Morelli (2004) follows the intuition of the standard efficiency-wage model in labor economics, in which the quality of applicants increases in the salary (Weiss 1980).
Another very interesting result of Caselli and Morelli (2004) is the following: Low-quality politicians generate a negative externality for high-quality politicians since the reputation of individual politicians is affected by the perceived overall quality of the pool of politicians. Due to this externality there can be multiple equilibria. For example, in low-quality ("bad") equilibria with many low-quality politicians, high-quality candidates face weak incentives to enter politics. A further interesting idea is the one of path dependence in quality. In endogenizing the rewards from political office, politicians can influence or manipulate (in the case of low-quality politicians) the rewards of political office for prospective politicians. This leads to the persistence of equilibria with either low-quality or high-quality politicians.

ulation size. They implement a fuzzy regression discontinuity design to use the discontinuities in pay to identify the causal effect of pay on selection. Intuitively, if the pay of politicians is smoothly associated to other characteristics at the population cut-offs, the effect of pay is estimated by comparing the selection of politicians in municipalities with population levels just below and above these thresholds.[13] As pay is not completely explained by the cut-offs, the fuzzy regression discontinuity design applies a two-stage least squares estimator using the indicators for the population cut-offs as first-stage instruments for the increases in pay. Their results indicate that higher pay improves the quality of candidates and elected politicians as approximated by education (average years of school attendance and the share with at least a high-school degree), previous profession (a higher fraction of politicians with high opportunity costs; i.e., more lawyers and businessmen are attracted) and previous political experience. Moreover, higher pay increases political competition indicated by more citizens who run for political office.

Gagliarducci and Nannicini (2012) provide consistent evidence in a similar empirical setting for Italian mayors for the period 1993 to 2001. Given that in Italy, it is the statutory pay and not a cap, which varies with population, they implement a sharp regression discontinuity design.[14] Comparing the observations lying closely on either side of the sharp population cut-off of 5,000 provides evidence that a higher salary attracts candidates with higher opportunity costs as approximated by years of schooling and a white collar professional background. This selection effect also translates into the elected mayors. Furthermore, the study exploits term limits in order to disentangle the selection and the incentive effects that pay has on in-office performance. Interestingly, most of the improved performance is driven by selection.[15]

Though being excellent contributions, one would like to understand the external validity of the obtained results; e.g., regarding (the reform of) the salary of national politicians. Monetary incentives may have the smallest relative importance at the national level since becoming a national politician is accompanied by more power and higher prestige.

Kotakorpi and Poutvaara (2011) analyze an increase in politicians' pay on the national level. They apply a differences-in-differences approach to an increase of 35% in Finnish parliamentary pay introduced in 2000. They find this increase to be associated with a larger fraction of candidates with higher education. This effect is, however, evident for women candidates only. Merlo et al. (2010) observe that the average quality of Italian parliamentarians in terms of formal education has decreased with increasing pay after World War II. However, they abstain from interpreting this result as causal since it is difficult to separate selection effects of pay increases from other confounding factors.

An innovative and closely related idea is presented by Gagliarducci et al. (2010) who examine the moonlighting activities of politicians. Assuming that the political mar-

13 For a discussion of the regression discontinuity design (RDD), see Imbens and Lemieux (2008).

14 A sharp RDD-design involves a deterministic cut-off at the threshold, around which there is a discontinuity in the probability of assignment from 0 to 1.

15 As indicated, both contributions also show that higher pay is related to more effort in office. Gagliarducci and Nannicini (2012) focus on budget indicators, whereas Ferraz and Finan (2009) concentrate on the bill sponsorship and the provision of public infrastructure.

ket and other markets are not mutually exclusive, high-quality candidates will be more likely to run when there is no restriction in terms of outside earnings. Entering politics is positively associated with gaining visibility and access to new networks, thus rendering a political office more attractive for high-quality candidates. However, a trade-off emerges: The high-quality candidates, once elected, will be less dedicated to their parliamentary duties as they prefer pursuing their private economic interests. Indeed, confronting these predictions with data for Italian parliamentarians between 1996 and 2006, they show that the marginal returns to quality (quality being approximated with previous market income) are enhanced after being elected. The ratio between outside income and pre-election income increases when moving up in the pre-election earnings quintiles and the respective coefficient is larger than one when regressing outside income on pre-election income. This indicates that high-quality candidates have a comparative advantage in terms of outside earnings. Regarding discipline in office, they find that parliamentarians with higher outside income are less committed to parliamentary activities as to voting attendance.[16]

Besides pay in office and outside earnings, the third major component for the monetary attractiveness of a political office is post-office returns. Two first contributions try to evaluate these monetary returns to holding a political office.

Based on career information on members of the U.S. congress between 1953 and 1994, Diermeier et al. (2005) find that congressional experience significantly increases post-office salaries in the private sector for Members of Congress. However, the marginal effect of an additional term in office on post-office income diminishes quite rapidly. Eggers and Hainmueller (2009) innovatively estimate the monetary returns to holding a parliamentary seat for recently deceased members of the British House of Commons who served between 1950 and 1970. They apply both a matching and a regression discontinuity design to compare elected parliamentarians with candidates who narrowly lost. They find that parliamentary service almost doubled the wealth of Conservative members of parliament, but had no financial benefits for members of parliament adhering to the Labour Party. As an explanation for the partisan bias they show that Conservative members of parliament profited from office mainly due to lucrative outside and post-office employments. For parliamentarians from the Labour Party they argue that trade unions were able to exert sufficient control over the party and its members of parliament to prevent them from selling their services to other clients.

Taken together, the theoretical contributions deliver opposing predictions on the relationship between pay and quality in politics. Based on rich micro data on local politicians, empirical work shows that a higher pay increases the ex-ante quality of candidates and elected politicians. Moreover, first contributions on outside and post-office earnings to politics suggest that these monetary returns also have to be taken into account when evaluating the attractiveness of a political office.

16 Regarding in-office effort Becker et al. (2009) show for members of the German parliament elected in the majoritarian tier of the electoral system that the more contested the electoral districts are, the less the politicians engage in outside activities.

2.2 Electoral rules and parties

In this section, we turn to the question of whether electoral rules systematically influence the selection of politicians. We center on the incentives that parties face in selecting candidates depending on the nature of competition in alternative electoral systems. Previous research has investigated the relationship between particular institutional features of the electoral system such as district magnitude, ballot structure and majoritarian versus proportional representation rules and different measures for political outcomes and policy choices. The research program by Persson and Tabellini (2005) serves as a benchmark in this line of research.[17] As to parties, the political economy literature has focused on examining the single party functions. These functions include, among others, the organization of electoral campaigns (e.g., Osborne and Tourkey 2008), the mobilization of voters (e.g., Herrera and Martinelli 2006), their informational role as intermediaries (e.g., Caillaud and Tirole 2002 as well as Snyder and Ting 2002), the choice of policy platforms (e.g., Levy 2004), and the disciplining of politicians (e.g., Alesina and Spear 1988).[18]

The impact of electoral rules and parties on political selection has just recently been addressed by political economists. Rather than analyzing the supply of politicians, the first contributions by Mattozzi and Merlo (2011) and Galasso and Nannicini (2011a,b) concentrate on the demand for politicians by parties. Alternative electoral rules are highly relevant as they are assumed to fundamentally change electoral competition and shape parties' incentives when selecting candidates.

Mattozzi and Merlo (2011) propose an equilibrium model of ex-ante selection by two competing parties. They show that competing parties may not choose to recruit and nominate the best candidates. Recruiting candidates of high quality enhances the electoral prospects of the party (the competition effect on selection). However, party organizations also hinge on the willingness of their members to exert effort in the various stages of the electoral process. In order to maximize the collective effort undertaken on behalf of the party (leaders), parties prefer to select mediocre but homogeneous and committed members as candidates. Thereby, the nomination as candidate is considered the reward for loyal party services. The selection of high-quality candidates might discourage other party members from providing political support to the party (discouragement effect on selection). In majoritarian electoral systems, an equilibrium with a selection of politicians of mediocre quality; i.e., average-quality is less likely. The more

17 With regard to the choice of redistributive politics under alternative electoral rules, important contributions are presented by Lizzeri and Persico (2001), Milesi-Ferretti et al. (2002) and Funk und Gathmann (2012). The relationship between electoral rules and corruption is analyzed; e.g., by Kunicová and Rose-Ackerman (2005) and Persson et al. (2003). Microeconomic evidence on the behavior of politicians under alternative electoral systems is scarce due to the paucity of available data sets. An exception is Gagliarducci et al. (2011) exploring the effect of the two-tier system of the Italian electoral rule on politicians' behavior.

18 For a discussion, see Merlo (2006) chapter 4.

candidate-centered and more competitive nature of the electoral process in majoritarian systems increases the electoral returns to selecting high-quality candidates.[19]

Galasso and Nannicini (2011a) take up the issue of parties strategically selecting and allocating candidates of heterogeneous quality depending on the intensity of political competition. In their theoretical model, two parties compete in a majoritarian electoral system. Each party first selects the share of candidates being either experts (high-quality candidates) or loyalists (low-quality candidates) depending on the degree of political competition. The former group is highly valued in terms of winning the election, but more costly for the parties.[20] In the second stage, parties allocate the experts; i.e., the high-quality candidates into the most contested electoral districts. Based on data on Italian parliamentarians between 1994 and 2006, the empirical evidence supports the beneficial effect of political competition on the selection and allocation of politicians. The closer electoral races in the districts are the more do parties rely on high-quality candidates, measured by years of schooling, previous market income and local government experience.[21]

Galasso and Nannicini (2011b) extend the previous framework to study the quality of politicians under alternative electoral rules. It is argued that differences in the average quality of politicians between majoritarian and proportional electoral systems critically depend on whether there are relatively many or few contested electoral districts in the former system. They, again, use Italy with its mixed-member electoral system to test this hypothesis. The preliminary findings are consistent with the hypothesis. The average quality of politicians (approximated by the same measures of ex-ante quality as in Galasso and Nannicini 2011a) in the majoritarian tier is higher than in the proportional tier if there is a large share of contested electoral districts. Put differently, the superiority of majoritarian systems with regard to the selection of high-quality politicians hinges on the degree of electoral competition.

3 Direct professional interest representation in politics

In this section, we turn our attention to one important quality dimension of politicians, namely their professional background. We select two prominent groups present in politics; i.e., businessmen and lawyers. In particular, we ask which conditions influence

19 So far, selection effects of electoral rules have been studied only with respect to the representation of women in politics. Norris and Franklin (1997) find that the fraction of women in parliaments is systematically higher under a proportional electoral rule (with closed lists) and with parties that have instituted formal gender quotas for candidate nomination. See De Paola et al. (2010) who report a positive selection effect of the introduction of party-list gender quotas on the representation of women in local politics in Italy.

20 Serna (1995) complementarily argues that one can think of the party calculus of selecting candidates also in the dimension of control costs. High-quality candidates are more likely to be successful in winning elections but may also generate higher costs in terms of a stronger incentive to deviate from the party leader's position. A low-quality candidate (in some models termed loyal) might be more easily aligned.

21 With regard to discipline, the study shows that politicians elected in close races display a lower absenteeism rate (as a proxy for shirking or rent-seeking). With the help of a regression discontinuity design, this effect is shown to be driven rather by selection than by incentives.

the attractiveness of a political mandate for these two groups and pay attention to the underlying institutional structure.

3.1 Businessmen in politics

To favor the proper business interests in politics, businessmen can either influence politicians by contributing to electoral campaigns or use political connections. With regard to the latter channel of political influence, a fast-growing research in finance and corporate finance analyzes the value of political connections for firm profitability. Politically connected firms are defined as having close connections to politics; most frequently by means of directly employing politicians. The evidence suggests that political connections are related to improved operational and stock market performance (see, e.g., Fisman 2001, Faccio 2006, 2010, Ferguson and Voth 2008, and Goldman et al. 2009) as well as preferential access to credit markets (see, e.g., Faccio et al. 2006 as well as Khwaja and Mian 2005). Political connections are found to be particularly attractive in weak institutional environments.[22]

All of these channels and mechanisms to exert political influence are, however, indirect. The most direct channel; i.e., businessmen running for political office themselves - a phenomenon quite frequently observed - has not been yet subject to much scholarly attention. Famous recent examples include Roman Abramovich being eight years the governor of a Russian region, Yulia Tymoshenko (former president of the Ukraine) and, of course, Silvio Berlusconi in Italy. On the one hand, businessmen in politics might bring in professional experience relevant to political decision-making. Moreover, given their outside activity, they may contribute to legislative decision making which is more independent from narrow party leaders' interests. On the other hand, consistent with the results presented by research on the value of political connections, businessmen might use the political office to primarily exert direct political influence and promote their private economic interests.

One interesting contribution is presented by Bunkanwanicha and Wiwattanakantang (2009). They look directly at "big" businessmen in politics. Complementary to the studies cited above, they find event study based evidence for Thailand that businessmen use the political office to further private economic ends. They show that the channel through which the businessmen's firms profit from the direct interest representation in politics is favorable regulation and the hindering of domestic and foreign competitors rather than preferential access to debt financing.

Gehlbach et al. (2010) ask under which institutional conditions businessmen run for office by themselves rather than rely upon other means of special interest influence.[23] In the theoretical model, they demonstrate that the incentives of businessman candidates to run for political office are weak when democratic institutions are relatively well de-

---

22 Most studies provide empirical evidence for East Asian countries with relatively underdeveloped institutional environments. Consistently, Faccio (2006) and Faccio and Parsley (2009) report for cross-country analyses that firm values are more responsive to political connections in more corrupt countries.

23 Related to considerations on post-office returns, one might also investigate the (institutional) conditions which render it more likely that politicians leave politics and work in the business sector instead.

veloped and high levels of political accountability do not allow for rent extraction in the political sphere. In contrast, when democratic institutions are weak businessmen can obtain rents in the political sphere. By running for office, they additionally avoid lobbying costs. Compared to other candidates, businessmen are assumed to face higher opportunity costs of running for political office as time and effort must be shifted from business to campaigning. If extractable rents from holding political office are very high, the opportunity costs of other (professional) politicians are lower. Accordingly, businessman candidates are crowded out of the race. Gehlbach et al. (2010) refer to Russian gubernational elections between 1991 and 2005 to provide empirical evidence. Consistent with the theoretical prediction they find that the likelihood of businessmen candidacy is decreasing in media freedom and government transparency (as proxies for strong democratic institutions). In order to test the crowding out of businessmen by (professional) politicians when there are weak democratic institutions that come with a high level of extractable rents, they study the differential effect of the fraction of employment in natural resource extraction industries (as a proxy for extractable rents) interacted with the development of democratic institutions. Only for regions with weak democratic institutions, do they find resource abundance to be associated with a decrease in the probability of businessmen running for political office.

Rosenson (2006) relates the representation of businessmen in politics to disclosure rules. She shows for the U.S. state legislatures that the stricter the rules of financial disclosure the lower the fraction of businessmen.

The same question, however, with another institutional focus is investigated by Li et al. (2006). They examine the impact of market, rather than political institutions on the direct (interest) representation of businessmen in politics. Similar to the literature on politically connected firms, they argue that entering politics is favorable to businessmen as it gives them decision-making power over issues that may concern their own firms. In addition, personal engagement in politics comes with new personal contacts to important government bureaucrats (who are often part of the same legislative body) facilitating access to preferential treatment. The weaker the political and market institutions the more businessmen (have to) rely on entering politics to pursue their economic interests. For China, they find businessmen to be more frequently represented in politics in regions where market and political institutions that support the functioning of markets are underdeveloped. The institutional environment is empirically approximated with the openness of the product and credit market, the intensity of state regulation, the informal tax burden and the availability of legal services as a measure of the faith in the rule of law.

In sum, the few existing contributions on the selection of businessmen into politics by Gehlbach et al. (2010), Rosenson (2006) and Li et al. (2006) indicate that the underlying institutional structure systematically influences the attractiveness of a political office for businessman candidates. The evidence presented can also be regarded as complementary to the results found in the literature on the value of political connections.

3.2 Lawyers in politics

Another prominent and strongly represented profession in politics is the group of lawyers. Considerations regarding the consequences of their direct representation reach from concerns of legislation biased towards the professional interests of lawyers to the idea of lawyers (with their particular educational training and professional experience) being close to the concept of politicians as fiduciaries.

Figure II.1 Representation of lawyers in selected national parliaments

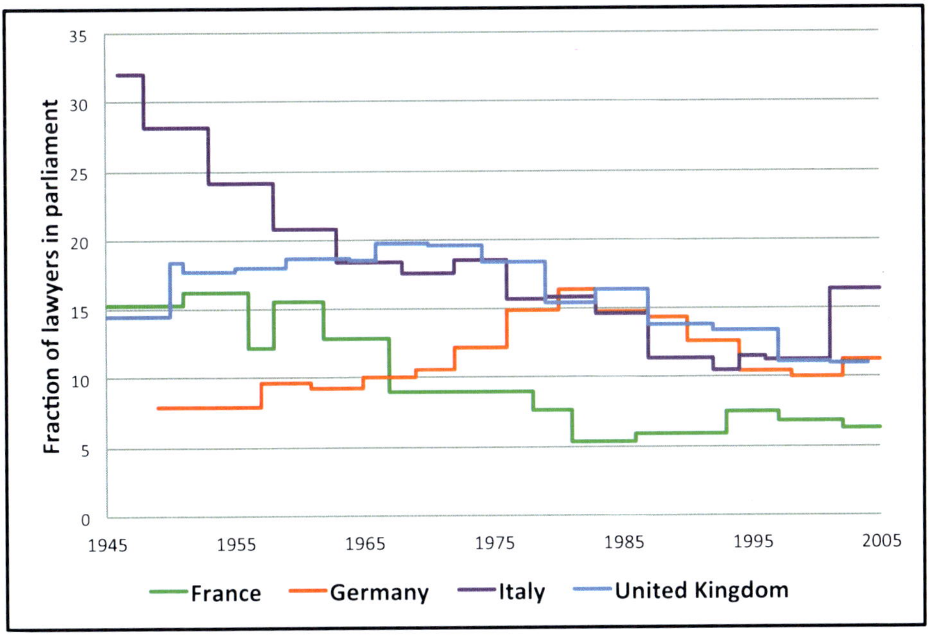

Notes: The figure is based on data provided by Cotta and Best (2007) who collect the information from national experts. The representation of lawyers in politics is measured as of the beginning of each legislative period.

Figure II.1 illustrates the representation of lawyers over time for the first parliamentary chambers of France, Germany, Italy and the United Kingdom. On the one hand, we observe substantial differences between the national parliaments. In 2005, for example, the fraction of legislators with a professional background in law is 16.3% in Italy, whereas the fraction in France is less than 7%. On the other hand, Figure II.1 indicates substantial variation in the representation of lawyers in politics over time. The strong representation of lawyers is a phenomenon also well known in U.S. politics. For example, the fraction of lawyers in the U.S. House of Representatives is 22.7% in 2008.[24]

24 The fraction of lawyers for the U.S. House of Representatives is based on own calculations.

Early contributions by U.S. political scientists, such as Schlesinger (1957), Hain and Pierson (1975), Podmore (1977), and more recently by Miller (1995) emphasize that the selection of lawyers into politics is mainly due to the compatibility of legal and political careers in terms of i) required competences and ii) time and local requirements. With respect to the former point, Norris and Lovenduski (1995) argue that lawyers belong to the group of "talking professions" who have more ease to enter politics. Even more so, law is often regarded a necessary prerequisite to become a politician. Woodrow Wilson (cited in Podmore 1977: 184), for instance, stated: "[T]he profession I chose was politics; the profession I entered was the law. I entered one because I thought it would lead to the other."

The recent theoretical considerations presented by Gagliarducci et al. (2010) and Mattozzi and Merlo (2008) might fit well for lawyers in politics.[25] Entering politics for a certain period (political careers) might be particularly attractive in terms of gaining visibility and access to new networks which help to promote private economic ends. The empirical analysis of Gagliarducci et al. (2010) for Italy shows - indicative of the latter argument – that lawyers have a comparative advantage in terms of outside earnings as they are among those politicians with (the highest absolute outside earnings and) the highest outside earnings compared to previous earnings. Moreover, since the legal profession is highly regulated a further argument is that politics is particularly attractive to lawyers in order to influence the legislation relevant to the own profession.

Rosenson (2006) draws on this reasoning and argues that stricter ethics laws, which include disclosure provisions and restrictions on outside earnings, add to the cost of running for political office and deter candidates that face substantial conflicts of interest, as is the case for lawyers and businessmen.[26] Based on a data set on the occupational composition of U.S. state legislatures, she finds that especially restrictions on the representation of clients before state entities as one facet of ethics laws are negatively related to the representation of lawyers. For financial disclosure rules, a negative – though not statistically significant – effect is found.[27]

Her analysis shows weaknesses as to employed data and the inclusion of control variables. For example, she simultaneously includes the fraction of lawyers in parliament and a variable covering the occupational diversity of parliament. Nevertheless, the contribution points to further interesting issues. In particular, it is empirically addressed whether the organizational structure of the legislature regarding time requirements and instituted independent ethics commissions influence the incentives for self-selection into politics.

---

25 The earliest contribution by economists which takes up the issue of lawyers in politics is McCormick and Tollison (1978). They argue that lower legislative pay (indicative of a part-time parliament) attracts more lawyers as it is more compatible with their outside activities. However, the focus of their analysis is on the determinants of legislative pay.

26 She also argues that stricter disclosure rules, which aim at enhancing transparency in politics, might have negative selection effects if high-quality candidates have a strong preference for privacy and the partisan and journalistic use of disclosed information makes public life unsatisfying.

27 van Aaken and Voigt (2011) find no effect of disclosure rules on the representation of lawyers at the country level.

4 Discussion

Quality of politicians

When we think of the pool of politicians as being endogenous, the questions of what defines a "good" or a high-quality politician and which characteristics matter most for being a "good" politician become major concerns. Earlier conceptions and especially agency-theoretic frameworks focus on ex-post quality; i.e., behavior in office. Thereby, being reelected is often used as a proxy for ex-post quality. A related dimension is to look at the actual policy choice of politicians in terms of congruence with citizens' preferences. Conceptually, one might think of a "good" politician as being one who implements the policy which would be preferred by the median voter or the policy that would be chosen behind a veil of uncertainty.[28] As discussed before, recent research mainly considers political quality as composed of honesty and competence. Honesty is undisputed to be a core characteristic, though, it is difficult to address (empirically). Competence is understood in terms of ex-ante competence and empirically approximated with measures such as educational attainment, previous income and profession and previous political experience. Whether these dimensions are the most relevant ones and in fact matter for delivering better policies is subject to ongoing research.

Institutional determinants of political selection

We pointed to the range of institutions that are relevant to the study of political selection and discussed in more detail how the salary paid to politicians, outside and post-office returns, and parties under alternative electoral rules impact the attractiveness of a political office.

As regards the comparative institutional analysis of restrictions on outside and post-office earnings, a point that deserves further attention is conflicts of interest. With (high) outside earnings, politicians face not only a conflict of time but also a conflict of interest. On the one hand, citizens desire politicians with experience outside politics. In addition, the possibility of outside earnings is likely to make politics a more attractive market to engage in for high-quality candidates. On the other hand, politicians earning more from outside employments in and consultancy contracts ("*Beraterverträge*") by large companies or interest groups than from parliamentary allowances face a conflict of interest and spark strong concerns regarding their independent political stance. An institutional arrangement which, to a certain degree, balances the countervailing forces is one which allows for outside earnings but with full disclosure.

Conflicts of interest due to outside earnings are more imminent and severe than those due to post-office returns. However, the concern that parliamentarians may become beholden to a government that has appointed them to certain posts after their election has led to incompatibility rules which are extended beyond the period of serving as a parliamentarian. It would be highly interesting to study in more detail the further causes

28 See Brennan and Buchanan (1985) for the latter concept.

for different institutional arrangements on outside and post-office earnings and whether these different rules do impact political discipline and selection.[29]

Electoral rules and parties

Regarding (ex-ante) selection, we emphasized the incentives faced by parties when recruiting candidates depending on the nature of competition in alternative electoral rules in Section 2.2. A promising direction for further research on selection by and within parties is the analysis of the relationship between differences in party nomination procedures and the quality of candidates. As basis might serve the pioneering work by Lundell (2004) and Hix (2004) who identify differences in the centralization of party nomination procedures in a comparative perspective for European countries.

Interaction of institutions

The theoretical and empirical analyses presented in this chapter mainly try to isolate and identify the effect that single institutions have on political selection. Future research has clearly to broaden the perspective and should entail a more detailed analysis of potential interactions between different institutional features. One might think of the differential selection effects of strict disclosure rules with a (more or less) independent media system or a (more or less) candidate-centered electoral rule. Another unexplored issue is the potential interaction between the organizational structure of a parliament regarding time requirements and the institutional provisions on moonlighting, disclosure and incompatibility rules. An interesting and unique combination of political institutions to consider is the Swiss institutional arrangement. It is characterized by a part-time parliament entailing a low pay, no restrictions on moonlighting, loose disclosure rules and soft incompatibility rules for public servants running for political office.

Direct interest representation in politics: Businessmen, lawyers and public servants

In the preceding section, we concentrated on the professional background as one important quality of politicians and discussed the selection of two prominent groups; i.e., businessmen and lawyers. The empirical evidence presented by Gehlbach et al. (2010) and Rosenson (2006) shows that especially institutions which serve to enhance transparency in politics, such as freedom of the media system and disclosure rules decrease the attractiveness of a political mandate for businessmen. Consistent with the literature on politically connected firms, the empirical evidence suggests that businessmen and lawyers enter politics to promote private economic interests. A further very interesting implication of the contribution by Gehlbach et al. (2010) is that whether personal engagement in politics is a complement or a substitute to influencing politics (either by

29 With respect to the analysis of institutional restrictions on post-office employment, a good point of departure is the literature on term limits (see e.g., Besley and Case 1995 and Lopez 2003).

sending lobbyists or directly paying politicians) also depends on the institutional environment.

When we continue to focus on the professional background, similar questions as addressed in the preceding section are to be applied to other prominent professional groups. For example, why do we observe such large numbers of farmers particularly in Swiss politics? Is the direct representation in politics one additional channel of political influence which helps to explain special interest politics such as highly persistent protectionist Swiss agricultural trade policies?
And, why do we observe so many educational professions in politics? Couch et al. (1992) argue that the private economic interests of educators who hold dual office in the educational sector and the legislature lead to inefficient allocation of public funds. For Alabama, they find that public funding per student at the junior and senior colleges that employ legislators as educators is significantly higher than that received by comparable institutions. Serna (1995) observes a positive relation between the representation of teachers in Swiss cantonal parliaments (the subnational level) and the pay of cantonal teachers.
And even more so, why are most national parliaments dominated by politicians with a public service background and which are the consequences for political processes and outcomes? Best and Cotta (2000) address the long-term trends in the educational and professional composition of parliaments.

As indicated in Figure II.2, the average fraction of public servants in the national parliaments of France, Germany, Italy and the United Kingdom is 38.7% in 2000, whereas it is only 27.4% in 1950. The fraction of public servants is lowest in the United Kingdom (1959); i.e., 13.3% and highest in France (1981); i.e., 53.8%. Best and Cotta (2000) argue that differences in the representation over time might be mainly induced by changing demands for political competence. Best et al. (2000) provocatively characterize public servants' representation as being "[d]istant from the productive sectors of the economy, the risks of the labor market and the pressure of competition in achievement-oriented work environments" but also as being specialized "[i]n redistribution rather than the creation of wealth" (p. 173). As a further explanation of their strong representation, they hint at the role of the particular institutional conditions candidates with a public sector background face. Yet, they abstain from systematically investigating causes and consequences. This is what the following chapters address in detail.

Figure II.2
Representation of public servants in selected national parliaments

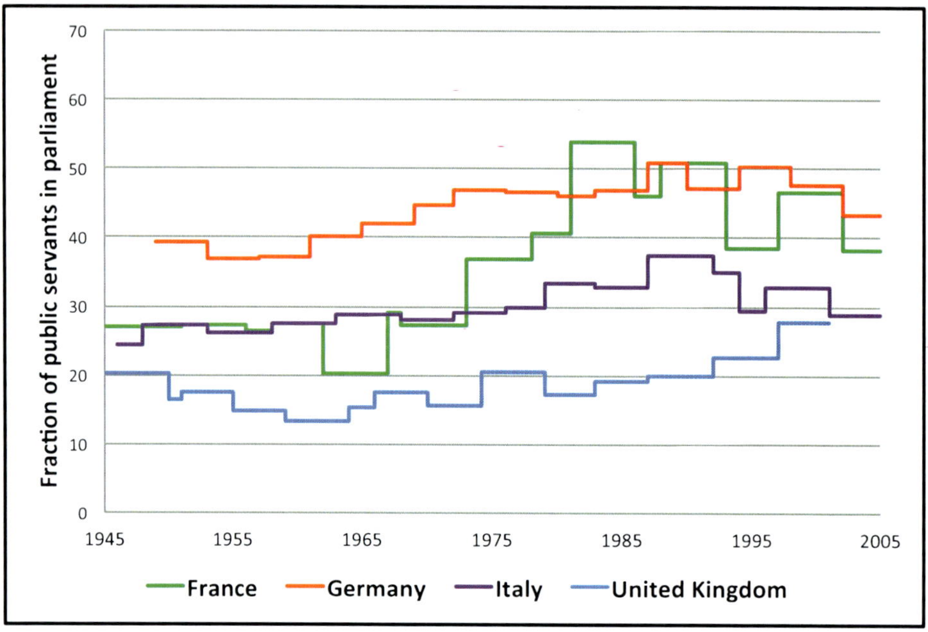

Notes: The figure is based on Cotta and Best (2007) who collect the information from national experts. The most recent values of the time-series are similar to the values found in the cross-country analysis in chapter III for the years 2000 to 2010. Differences might be due to different research objectives or other sources. The representation of public servants in politics is measured as of the beginning of the legislative period.

Chapter III: Selection of Public Servants into Politics: A First Pass*

1 Introduction

The identity of politicians matters for the political process and good government. This seems to be self-evident as political control and the credibility of policy commitments in the democratic process are limited. A careful selection of representatives is thus important to bring the outcomes of the political process as closely as possible in line with citizens' preferences when delegating decision-making power. Obviously, the pool of people who consider pursuing a career in politics is very heterogeneous with regard to ideals and interests, as people differ in their gender, religious orientation, and education.

We focus on the identity of politicians in terms of their professional backgrounds. This is important, firstly, for determining the personal socio-economic conditions that influence an individual's decision to run for office. Secondly, it shapes their private economic interests influencing the behavior once elected. Some of these interests are mediated by links to professional interest or lobby groups. Thirdly, the specialist knowledge and expertise of certain professions are essential in the parliamentary process.

In this chapter, we concentrate on the single largest professional group present in most national legislatures; i.e., the parliamentarians who are recruited from the public sector. This group poses a major challenge when assessing political selection into national legislatures for two main reasons. First, the instatement of politicians from the public sector presents two important issues: interest representation and professional expertise. On the one hand, their double role as agents in public service and as principals that supervise the executive branch in parliament compromises the (personal) separation of powers. This generates a conflict of interest.[1] On the other hand, politicians with a public service background embody independence from specific business interests. Furthermore, they constitute a pool of people with first-hand information on public service issues and a revealed interest in these matters. Accordingly, where public servants in parliament are made accountable to the electorate, their valuable expertise may even serve as a check in the oversight process. Second, many countries have instituted specific rules for this professional group which aim to prevent inherent conflicts of interest. These rules either specify the incompatibility of a public sector position with a legislative mandate or even declare public servants ineligible for candidacy. We hypothesize that these rules systematically change the pool of available candidates and elected politicians.

We pursue three goals with our contribution. First, we aim to document the phenomenon of the strong representation of public servants in national legislatures. We present a newly compiled data set on the composition of the first parliamentary cham-

* This chapter is based on joint work with Alois Stutzer. It is a refined version of the WWZ Discussion Paper No. 06/11 with the title "Selection of Public Servants into Politics".

1 Only a few public choice academics do have commented on this concern (e.g., Tullock 1965 and Frey and Pommerehne 1982).

ber in 71 countries for the years 2000 to 2010. Interestingly, there are large differences in the fraction of members with a public sector background. In the UK, for example, the fraction is 23%, while it is 49% in Denmark. Second, we analyze the determinants of the variation in their representation. In particular, we study legal provisions that primarily aim to inhibit conflicts of interest; i.e., the different regimes that define and deal with the (in)compatibility of public service employment with a mandate in the legislature. Accordingly, data is collected on the (in)compatibility regimes for the same 71 countries. It is hypothesized that incompatibility provisions reduce the attractiveness of a political mandate and are thus related to a lower fraction of public servants in parliament. Third, an initial basis is provided to explore the consequences that a strong representation of public servants in national parliaments has on the political process. We explore the relationship between the political selection of public servants and corruption as well as the size of the government sector.

As main results, we find that the average fraction of politicians with a public sector background is 31% in our sample. With regard to incompatibility rules, we observe six countries with a compatibility regime, 23 countries with a soft incompatibility, and 37 countries with a strict incompatibility regime. Five countries apply an ineligibility rule. The application of stricter incompatibility rules (strict incompatibility or ineligibility), signifying higher opportunity costs of a political mandate, is statistically related to a smaller fraction of public servants in parliament by roughly seven percentage points. This difference is robust to a series of sensitivity checks for potentially correlated economic and institutional conditions as well as for sample restrictions. The difference is even larger if countries with a compatibility regime are compared to countries where ineligibility rules are in force. Regarding the supplementary evidence for political outcomes, we find that the fraction of public servants in parliament is statistically significantly correlated with a lower level of corruption and a higher level of government consumption. While we consider these correlations interesting as such, causal relationships may go either way. Two-stage estimations using the incompatibility regime as an instrument lead to coefficients for the political selection variable of similar size but with larger standard errors.

Section 2 presents the rationale for (in)compatibility rules from a historical perspective and derives hypotheses regarding the representation of public servants in national parliaments. In Section 3, we, first, provide a detailed description of the compiled dataset. Second, we lay out our econometric analysis and show the partial correlations between the institutional factors and the political selection of public servants. Section 4 supplements the analysis with an explorative study on the consequences of the political selection of public servants for political outcomes; i.e., perceived corruption and government consumption. Section 5 offers concluding remarks.

2 The rationale and some history behind (in)compatibility regimes

In a democracy, government functions are usually assigned to different bodies. This separation of powers is pursued in order to reduce conflicts of interest and prevent the abuse of sovereign authority. Interestingly, the separation of powers principle is implemented rather differently with regard to individual people being allowed to hold multiple offices. One major constitutional decision coping with the alleviation of inherent (intrapersonal) conflicts of interest is the degree of compatibility of employment in the public sector with election to legislative assemblies.[2]

2.1 A short recapitulation of (in)compatibility regimes

Rules that declare employment in the public service incompatible with parliamentary mandates have been justified for three main reasons.[3]

First, incompatibility rules should prevent legislative assemblies from being composed of persons who are subject to government control due to their ties to the state or their economic dependence on it. This rationale dates back to eighteenth-century Britain and has aimed at protecting the independence of parliament from the strong influence of the crown. In the United Kingdom, this concern is (still) reflected in the House of Commons Disqualification Act of 1975. The latter act constitutes the basis for the ineligibility rule that still holds today.[4] A second motivation for introducing incompatibility or even ineligibility provisions is the concern that the public service will become politicized by allowing public servants to assume seats in parliament; where the public service is supposed to be an institution above the political arena. The enactment of tight restrictions on the political activity of public servants in the United States, for example, is explained mainly by the desire to maintain the (party-)political neutrality of the public service. These restrictions date back to the 19th century and were defined in the Civil Service Act of 1883 for the first time. These provisions were reassessed in the Hatch Act which still holds today.[5] In the 20th century, a third reason arose: Rules of incompatibility should protect the independence of the parliament by preventing the legislature from being dominated by people with public sector backgrounds and thus public service interests. The latter rationale became the predominant argument underlying the

2 Besides this major incompatibility, there are also restrictions for holding simultaneously more than one elected office. For example, the logic of bicameralism implies the restriction of the simultaneous holding of a seat in the first and second chamber of a democracy. The same rationale applies to incompatibilities between different federal levels (i.e., a mandate in the national parliament and in a regional assembly). Some European countries impose the same rules to prohibit seats being held jointly in the European Parliament and the national assembly. Moreover, incompatibilities of a ministerial office and parliamentary duties are the general rule in presidential regimes and are a characteristic feature of them. They are; e.g., found in countries like Brazil, Portugal, the United States and Switzerland.

3 For a detailed description of the historical evolution of incompatibility rules and for discussions from a comparative constitutional law perspective, see Tsatsos (1970) and Sturm (1967).

4 In some instances, the concern that parliamentarians may become beholden to a government that has appointed them to certain posts after their election has led to incompatibility rules which are extended beyond the period of serving as a parliamentarian. Thus, a similar argument applies as is the case with revolving door arrangements for regulators. In the United States, for example, no member of Congress may be appointed to an administrative office that has been created or for which the salary has been granted during his or her term of office. A similar incompatibility rule exists in the Philippines.

5 For a discussion from an administrative science point of view, see Bowman and West (2009), and Miller (2010).

constitutional design of the separation of powers relating to public servants elected to parliament.
Today, almost all democracies adhering to the principle of separation of powers stipulate some rules of incompatibility in their constitutional provisions.
In some countries, there is a movement to extend these rules of incompatibility to occupations beyond the public sector. In France and Italy, for example, holding a parliamentary mandate is incompatible with being a public contractor or a major supplier of public goods and services, or being the employee of a former public enterprise. Such rules mostly apply to management staff. Furthermore, in some countries incompatibility rules also restrict lawyers from continuously receiving mandates from public authorities, as is the case with Belgium. There are also countries that have legislation enforcing the incompatibility of a political mandate with employment in foreign enterprises or international organizations. This is the case in Egypt, for example. In general, however, the incompatibility rules that address types of private sector employment constitute exceptions.[6]

2.2 Selection effects of incompatibility rules

The conditions under which candidates with a public service background are allowed to take office in a legislature and the conditions they face as members of legislatures shape their incentives to run for a parliamentary mandate.[7] The relative attractiveness of such political mandates to public servants compared to private sector candidates is reflected in the fraction of public servants in parliament.

The law may declare that parliamentary membership is incompatible with a position in the public service. This obliges candidates, once elected, to relinquish their public service office. If public servants face an ineligibility rule, they are obliged to resign prior to running for the political mandate and risk having neither a seat in the legislative assembly nor a position in the public service. This increases the opportunity cost of running for a political mandate.

In contrast to ineligibility, rules of incompatibility constitute weaker restrictions. With strict incompatibility, all public servants have to hold their office in abeyance but may remain in office until they are elected for a mandate; they have guaranteed reemployment (in varying degrees) subsequent to the termination of their mandate.

With soft incompatibility, only some categories of public servants are restricted, whereas all other public servants can continue in their public service career, often with a guaranteed reduced workload. Some countries confine incompatibilities only to specific public offices, regardless of the rank in the hierarchy. In other countries, the ban affects only high-ranking public servants. While strict incompatibility increases the opportunity costs for all public servants, soft incompatibility increases costs only for some of them.

6 For a general discussion of various legal aspects of a parliamentary mandate from a comparative perspective, see van der Hulst (2000).

7 An overview of candidacy requirements for legislative elections in a set of countries is provided in Massicotte et al. (2004).

If a compatibility regime is applied, public servants elected to the legislature are free to juggle with their job in the public sector. In most cases, they face favourable conditions in terms of pay and time.

In sum, we expect that the stricter the incompatibility rule applied is, the higher will be the opportunity costs for public servants running for a political mandate. Accordingly, we expect to find the smallest fraction of citizens with a public sector background elected to parliaments in countries where ineligibility rules are in force.[8]

3 Empirical analysis for the political selection of public servants

3.1 Data

The empirical analysis is based on a newly collected dataset. It captures the fraction of public servants in 71 national parliaments for recent elections between 2000 and 2010 and the rules of (in)compatibility applied in the respective countries.[9]

Occupational composition of national legislatures

For recent single election periods, many occupational statistics are published by the Inter-Parliamentary Union (IPU) based on information supplied by parliamentary information services. The IPU tries to make the information comparable across countries. We adopted the fraction of public servants in parliament for 61 countries from this source. For another ten parliaments, we collected data from parliamentary online services. They either offer databases or systematic information about individual politicians' professions prior to entering parliament. Whenever more detailed information was available on the national parliamentary service web pages, we gave it preference over the information supplied by the IPU.[10] We consider the following occupational titles as public servants or employees of the public sector: teacher, professor, educational profession, researcher, scientist, civil or public servant and employee of the local, state or federal authority administration, judge, public prosecutor, employee of the judiciary, armed services or military, police official, social worker, and employee of a public enterprise (if indicated). Two typical examples for the IPU statistics present the occupational composition of the United Kingdom House of Commons elected in 2005 in Table A.1a

---

8 In some countries, public servants facing incompatibility restrictions are compensated with specific privileges. Guaranteed reemployment is the most important and widespread one. In France, for example, public servants, once elected to parliament, get a special status *(position de détachment)* which assures that they can return to a position (at least) equivalent to the one they left. Another privilege is the compensation for holding the public office in abeyance. Further specific privileges are discussed in chapter IV for the institutional context of the German subnational parliaments. In the current setting, we have to abstract from these institutions owing to information costs.

9 For the empirical analysis, it would have been desirable to also get access to some longitudinal data in order to identify effects of constitutional changes. However, there neither is comparable information available on the occupational composition for earlier legislative periods for a sufficient number of national parliaments nor do fundamental reforms of incompatibility regimes take place frequently.

10 For the U.S., no systematic information on the occupational background of the members of congress is available. We therefore coded information retrieved from various sources; i.e., in particular, the homepages of individual parliamentarians and the site "votesmart.org".

and the Algerian parliament elected in 2007 in Table A.1b in the Appendix.[11] For the United Kingdom, the statistic indicates that 140 out of 615 members (i.e., a fraction of 22.8%) have a public service occupational background. Of these members, 98 hold a position in the educational or research sector. 28 indicate a prior employment in the public administration and 14 members indicate military service or police service as occupation held prior to entering parliament. The background of the remaining 475 members are linked to eleven categories in the private sector, one category of professions related to political activities and one category for others. More detailed information offers the occupational statistic of the German parliamentary online service for the 17th German parliament (*Bundestag*) elected in 2009 (see Table A.1c in the Appendix). It indicates that 199 out of 622 members (i.e., a fraction of 32%), have a public sector background. Of these 199 members, 86 (43.2%) hold a position in the educational and research sector. The other 113 members hold the following functions: administration (62 members or 31.2%), judiciary (13 members or 6.5%), municipal public servants (13 members or 6.5%), medical professions (9 members or 4.5%), police (7 members or 3.5%), military service (3 members or 1.5%) and 3% execute other functions in the public service.

On average, the fraction of public servants elected to the 71 national parliaments in our sample is 31.4%. This number takes into account that in many statistics there is a category of parliamentarians with unknown professional background. The adjusted fraction is expressed relative to those politicians whose occupation is specified. The unadjusted or raw fraction is 29.4% in the sample. The fraction is lowest in Singapore in 2001 with 6.5% (unadj. 6%) and highest in Djibouti in 2008 with 73.9%. A complete list of the data sources and the fraction of public servants for every country is provided in Table A.2 in the Appendix. Table A.3 in the Appendix provides supplementary information on the subcategories in the individual countries as collected by the IPU.

In collecting and compiling data on the fraction of public servants in parliament, we encountered several methodological challenges. First, existing statistics on the socio-economic composition of parliaments differ as to their intended purpose. In contrast to our study, which concentrates on the last occupation held before election to parliament, some national statistics focus more on educational background, or occupation learned.[12,13] Second, if the statistics did not contain one coherent category for the public sector, we had to rearrange or to aggregate categories in order to gain comparable data. A frequent case is separate categories for members of parliament who are from the judicial branch, the administration, the education or the public security sector. For some of the countries, it is not clear which professions or functions belong to or are executed by the public service. Due to the variation in the degree of differentiation, we abstained from a refined data collection and generated aggregate data on the fraction of

11 The information about the United Kingdom House of Commons is very similar to the one provided by the national parliamentary service.

12 This is; e.g., the case for Canada, Bulgaria and Slovenia. In the case of Canada, we were able to retrieve the correct information based on the study of individual MPs' curricula vitae.

13 When analyzing individual curricula vitae, we encountered unclear chronologies of apportionments or the holding of multiple jobs at the same time (especially for members of the U.S. congress).

public servants. Countries for which the available information did not permit an expert judgment were excluded.

Institutional conditions
Rules of incompatibility are written down either in the national constitution, the electoral law or in one of the various laws governing the parliament, the judiciary and the public service. We are not aware of any study that systematically compares (in)compatibility regimes across countries. For the present study, we mainly collected and coded information provided by the IPU. Where no information was available (or where the information was contradictory), we looked for national provisions as far as information was available in English, German, Italian, or Spanish. We coded four different types of (in)compatibility or ineligibility regimes:

Ineligibility is given if all public servants have to resign from public service when they decide to become a candidate.
Strict incompatibility is given if all public servants have to hold their office in abeyance while in parliament.
Soft incompatibility is given if only some categories of public servants have to hold their office in abeyance while in parliament.
Compatibility is given if public servants elected to parliament may stay in their public service office.
In preparation of the empirical analysis, the four regimes are coded as dummy variables. Table A.4 in the Appendix gives an overview of the institutional conditions holding in each country as well as the data sources.
Two challenges in collecting the data on the incompatibility regimes have to be mentioned. First, the countries' information supplied to the IPU differ in amount and detailedness. In preparation of the empirical analysis, we therefore limit our coding to four general regimes. Second, depending on the (democratic) regime, the enforcement of political institutions in general and of incompatibility rules in particular might differ. We address this issue restricting the sample to more democratic regimes which are supposed to have a stronger adherence to the rule of law.

3.2 Results

(In)compatibility regimes are expected to modify the attractiveness of a political mandate for public servants and thus systematically affect the (self-)selection of citizens with different professional backgrounds into national parliaments. First, raw evidence is presented in Figure III.1. It shows the fraction of public servants elected under different (in)compatibility regimes in the period 2000 to 2010. Consistent with the theoretical hypothesis, the stricter the incompatibility rule applied is, the lower is the fraction of public servants elected to parliament. For the compatibility regime, we observe a fraction of public servants in parliament of 38.9% on average in the full sample. With soft incompatibility, the respective fraction is 34.4%. With strict incompatibility or ineligibility, 28.7%, and 28.5% respectively, are observed on average. A similar picture

Figure III.1
(In)compatibility regimes and the fraction of public servants in national parliaments

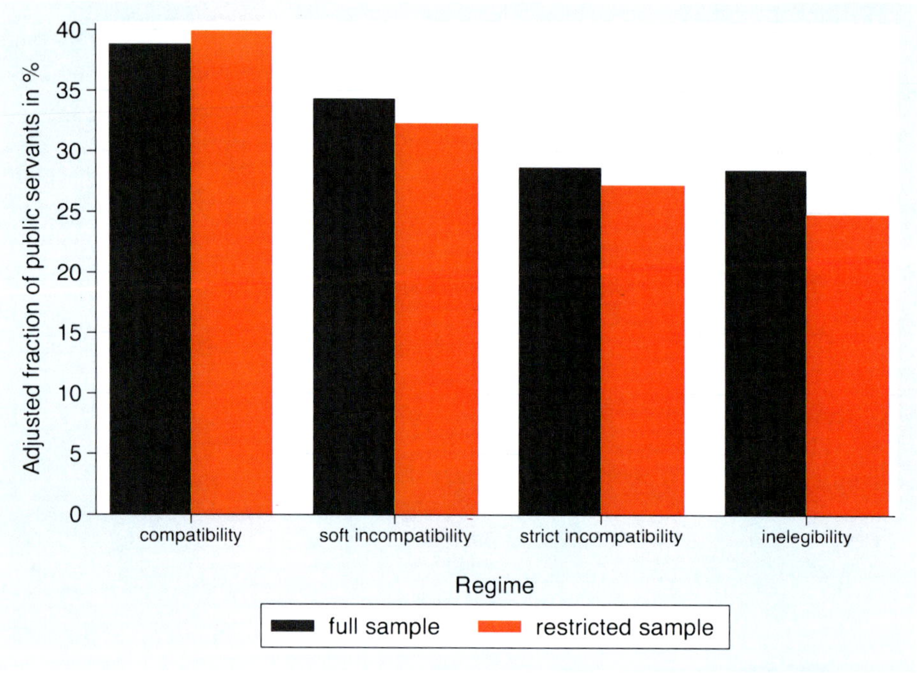

Notes: Information for 71 countries within the period 2000 to 2010 is included for the full sample. 59 countries are included in the sample restricted to "at least partly free democracies" according to the Freedom House democracy rating.
Sources: Own calculations based on IPU and national parliamentary data services.

emerges if we restrict the sample to at least partly free democracies (according to the Freedom House democracy rating).

In order to deal with correlated and confounding factors that might drive the raw correlation, the remainder of the empirical analysis focuses on the partial correlations from multiple regressions between institutional conditions for public servants as members of parliament and their actual representation in them. We report the results for a series of estimation specifications in order to uncover as much information as possible about our data pool. In particular, we test the robustness of our results including and excluding various control variables for institutional and economic development. In addition, we take into account a refined categorization of (in)compatibility regimes and restrict

Table III.1
Determinants of the representation of public servants in national parliaments
Dependent variable: Adjusted fraction of public servants (%)

	I	II	III
Strict incompatibility or ineligibility	–6.607**	–7.293**	–7.136**
	(3.18)	(3.13)	(3.15)
Ln(GDP per capita)		–1.801**	–1.166
		(0.88)	(1.25)
Democracy rating			–0.881
			(1.22)
No. of obs.	71	71	71
R^2	.059	.113	.120
Prob. > *F*	0.041	0.017	0.035

Notes: OLS estimations. Standard errors in parentheses. Adjustment of the dependent variable due to the category "unknown professions".
Significance levels: * $.05 < p < .1$, ** $.01 < p < .05$, *** $p < .01$.
Sources: See Tables A.2–A.5.

the sample once to "at least partly free democracies" and once to "free democracies" (according to the democracy rating published by Freedom House).

The first set of results in Table III.1 is based on the full sample of 71 countries. Panel I reports the results of a cross-sectional ordinary least squares estimation. In correspondence with Figure III.1, a strict incompatibility or an ineligibility rule is related to a 6.6 percentage points smaller fraction of public servants in parliament (the reference regime being compatibility or soft incompatibility). Panel II adds the log of GDP per capita in 2005 as a control variable for economic development. Panel III includes the Freedom House democracy rating of 2000 to control for the development of democratic institutions in general. Both control variables show no clear correlation with the fraction of public servants in national parliaments. The partial correlation for the variable capturing the (in)compatibility regimes remains almost unchanged.

The robustness of the partial correlations is studied in Table III.2. In panels II to IV, we analyze whether the (in)compatibility regimes are just place holders for other specific institutions (observed and unobserved), which are the actual drivers of occupation-specific political selection. Panel I repeats the baseline estimation. We concentrate on the voting system, disclosure rules and the legal origins. The variables are described in Table A.5 in the Appendix.

In a majority voting system, public servants who aspire to a political career might be in an advantageous position relative to competitors from the private sector. This is the case if they have already gained some prominence due to their position in the public service or if they benefit from flexible work conditions during their campaign. Accord-

Table III.2
Robustness analysis for alternative institutional and economic determinants of political selection
Dependent variable: Adjusted fraction of public servants (%)

	I	II	III	IV	V	VI
Strict incompatibility or ineligibility	–7.136**	–6.810**	–6.787**	–6.856*	–6.642**	–8.406**
	(3.15)	(3.14)	(3.37)	(3.48)	(3.25)	(3.24)
Ln(GDP per capita)	–1.166	–1.164	–0.386	–0.875	–1.347	–2.386
	(1.25)	(1.24)	(1.33)	(1.35)	(1.30)	(2.56)
Democracy rating	–0.881	–0.465	0.107	–0.870	–1.260	–0.523
	(1.22)	(1.25)	(1.44)	(1.33)	(1.28)	(1.24)
Majority voting system		4.827				
		(3.50)				
Disclosure rule index			–9.950			
			(7.13)			
UK legal origin				–0.965		
				(4.20)		
German legal origin				–2.500		
				(4.96)		
Scandinavian legal origin				9.726		
				(8.81)		
Fraction of women in parliament					0.213	
					(0.19)	
Fraction of employment in services sector						0.360
						(0.24)
No. of obs.	71	71	65	67	69	53
R^2	.120	.145	.132	.138	.126	.181
Prob. > *F*	0.035	0.033	0.070	0.162	0.069	0.044

Notes: OLS estimations. Standard errors in parentheses. The dependent variable is adjusted for the category "unknown professions" in national statistics. The reference category in panel II is a proportional or a mixed-member electoral system. In panel IV, the reference category is French legal origin.
Significance levels: * $.05 < p < .1$, ** $.01 < p < .05$, *** $p < .01$.
Sources: See Tables A.2–A.5.

ingly, we might expect a larger fraction of public servants to be represented in national parliaments.[14] If the same countries apply majority voting and soft incompatibility, the observed correlation in Table III.1 might be spurious. While a majority voting system is positively correlated with the fraction of public servants in national parliaments (though not statistically significantly), the partial correlation for the incompatibility variable remains robust in panel II.

If politicians have to disclose the sources of their outside income, a political mandate might become less attractive. This might, in particular, hold for public servants' competitors from the private sector; e.g., lawyers and businessmen. In order to control for this potentially correlated institutional feature of legislatures, we include a disclosure rule index for income sources (Djankov et al. 2010) in the regression estimation in panel III. Contrary to the reasoning above, we find no effect. The effect for the incompatibility variable is almost unchanged.

There are potentially many democratic institutions that affect the (self-)selection of public servants into national parliaments - institutions that might also be correlated with the (in)compatibility regimes. If these institutions are part of a bundle of institutions that follow a specific legal tradition, we can control for these unobserved factors by including legal origins as control variables (La Porta et al. 2008). Panel IV reports the results. Compared to countries with a French legal origin, countries with a Scandinavian legal origin have a sizeably larger fraction of public servants in national parliaments (though imprecisely measured). Legal origin, however, does not explain the negative partial correlation for strict incompatibility and ineligibility.

In the last two panels of Table III.2, we control for additional indicators of socio-economic development. In panel V, we test whether a gender-specific selection into parliament systematically affects the professional composition. Concretely, women are often employed in various public sector branches, such as the educational sector, public health or the social services. Thus, the selection of women into parliaments might systematically affect the representation of public servants. However, if we include the fraction of women elected into national parliaments in 2005, we find no corresponding empirical evidence.

In panel VI, the sectoral structure of an economy is taken into account. It might be hypothesized that an economy with a large service sector requires more state coordination. Correspondingly, more candidates from the public sector might be recruited for a political mandate. In our robustness test, we find a positive (though not statistically significant) partial correlation between the fraction of employment in the service sector and the fraction of public servants in parliament. The partial correlation for the incompatibility variable remains robust.

Table III.3 reports further robustness checks. First, we disaggregate the incompatibility indicator into the categories soft incompatibility, strict incompatibility and ineligibility. Panel II reports the finding next to the result of the baseline estimation in panel I.

14 However, if a candidacy in a majority voting system requires more resources because it is more focused on the individual candidates (relative to the parties), public servants might be at a disadvantage relative, e.g., to businessmen from the private sector.

Table III.3
Robustness analysis for a disaggregated (in)compatibility indicator and sample restrictions
Dependent variable: Adjusted fraction of public servants (%)

	I	II	III	IV	V	VI
Strict incompatibility or ineligibility	–7.136**		–7.360**		–6.219*	
	(3.15)		(3.55)		(3.63)	
Soft incompatibility		–4.607		–7.584		–14.786**
		(6.05)		(6.74)		(6.18)
Strict incompatibility		–10.732*		–13.345**		–17.204***
		(5.76)		(6.48)		(5.90)
Ineligibility		–10.907		–13.539		–19.104**
		(7.98)		(9.90)		(8.32)
Ln(GDP per capita)	–1.166	–1.036	–1.241	–1.233	–0.201	0.115
	(1.25)	(1.28)	(1.04)	(1.08)	(1.37)	(1.33)
Democracy rating	–0.881	–1.014				
	(1.22)	(1.25)				
No. of obs.	71	71	59	59	40	40
R^2	.120	.128	.085	.106	.073	.205
Prob. > *F*	0.035	0.106	0.082	0.186	0.244	0.083

Notes: OLS estimations. Standard errors in parentheses. The dependent variable is adjusted for the category "unknown professions" in national statistics. The reference category in panels II, IV and VI is a compatibility regime. Panel III and IV (V and VI) restrict the sample to "at least partly free democracies" ("free democracies") according to the Freedom House democracy rating.
Significance levels: * $.05 < p < .1$, ** $.01 < p < .05$, *** $p < .01$.
Sources: See Tables A.2–A.5.

The reference category is now a compatibility rule. In comparison, soft incompatibility is related to a 4.8 percentage points smaller fraction of public servants in parliament. For strict incompatibility the coefficient is -10.9 percentage points, and for ineligibility the coefficient is -11.2 percentage points, respectively. The effects for the refined categorization, however, are statistically precisely measured only in the case of strict incompatibility.

Second, we twice assess the robustness of our results: Once we restrict our sample to "at least partly free democracies" (panels III and IV) and once to "free democracies" (panels V and VI) according to the Freedom House democracy rating. We expect a stronger adherence to the rule of law in more democratic regimes. Correspondingly, the enforcement of political institutions in general, and of incompatibility rules in particular, is expected to be more stringent in the restricted sample of countries.[15] The estimations confirm the negative partial correlations between the strictness of the incompatibility rule and the representation of public servants. In particular, we find statistically significant negative partial correlations with larger effect sizes if the sample is restricted to free democracies.

In sum, the different (in)compatibility regimes are correlated with the fraction of public servants in a statistically robust way. The findings indicate that stricter incompatibility rules increase the opportunity costs of a political mandate for public servants and thus systematically affect political selection into national parliaments.

4 Consequences for political outcomes

4.1 The trade-off between conflicts of interest and competence

We differentiate between two channels through which rules of incompatibility affect political outcomes. First, incompatibility rules explicitly prohibit the simultaneous execution of an executive function and a legislative mandate. This constraint reduces intrapersonal conflicts of interest for public servants assuming a parliamentary seat. The incompatibility rule can thus be considered an (ex-ante) sanctioning device. Second, the same rules reduce conflicts of interest through their effect on political selection. As argued above, the stricter the rules in force are, the higher will be the opportunity costs of becoming a politician for candidates with a public sector background. If the arguments are restricted to conflicts of interest, we expect a more efficient provision of public goods and services with strict incompatibility owing to either its sanctioning effect, its effect on political selection, or both.

However, a trade-off emerges when we take into account the aspect of expertise in political selection. Public servants form a pool of people with first-hand information about public service issues and a revealed interest in these matters. If this competence pool is partly excluded from the parliamentary process, we alternatively can expect a

15 Applying the same reasoning to the institutional and economic determinants analyzed in Table III.2, we find very similar results for the sample restricted to "at least partly free democracies". The results are presented in Table A.6 in the Appendix.

less efficient government sector. We briefly develop these countervailing arguments related to political selection in more detail and derive specific testable hypotheses.

The concern for conflicts of interest rests on the personal union and affiliations between the legislative and executive body as well as the perk of guaranteed reemployment. In particular, the private interests of public servants might lead to slack that is less forcefully counteracted by committees that are largely composed of public servants. A case in point is their involvement in drafting and revising civil service law. Moreover, public servants are likely to have an information advantage with regard to legislative procedures. This allows for more leeway to manoeuvre, especially in areas they are professionally acquainted with such as administration, security, public finance or education.[16] As proponents and representatives of the public service, they may also favor policy choices that grant more competencies to the state and provide more services through the public sector, resulting in a larger government sector. In sum, a strong representation of public servants in parliament is expected to result in a large government sector and fewer countermeasures against misbehavior in the public service; e.g., in terms of corruption.

The competence argument emphasizes that politics is not simply a platform for the exchange of private interests. The expert knowledge possessed by public servants rather contributes to productive policy choices in parliament.[17] Public servants in parliament might also affect political outcomes simply due to their ties with the state. The vocation of a career in the public service might reflect particular loyalty to an organization set up to provide public services.[18] Given that public servants enjoy institutional privileges, such as reemployment guarantees and often favourable terms for leave of absence, they might be considered relatively independent of outside pressure and free to dedicate themselves to parliamentary duties until the end of their mandate. These aspects of the representation of public servants in parliament are particularly attractive if the information asymmetry between the executive and the legislative branch is severe (as stressed by Niskanen 1971). Electing insiders to parliament who become accountable to the elec-

16 This is not to say, that other members of parliament would not also pursue their own goals (and thus experience conflicts of interest). However, the authority of the legislature with regard to the duties of the public sector and the conditions governing public service are more concrete and immediate than for the private sector. Many aspects are more explicitly and more comprehensively regulated than in any other regulated market. While there are specific ordinances, e.g., regulating the business of pharmacies or the fees of attorneys, there are a multitude of laws and ordinances regulating the public service such as its internal training, pay, pension scheme and legal status.

17 Please note that there are substantial differences with respect to public servants' expertise of public service issues depending on their branch, function and position within the public service. We think, however, that all the members of parliament who were recruited from the public sector have at least some public service specific knowledge. First, this knowledge is with regard to the specific function they executed. Second, it is with regard to the general functioning of the public service as a whole. Of particular importance is the knowledge about the legal status of public servants, i.e., civil service salary law, civil service career law, public services law as well as the familiarity with the performance oversight executed by the public employer and ultimately by the parliament.

18 Public servants are more likely to donate money and blood to charities or to volunteer than employees in the private sector (Houston 2006). Public sector employees are also more likely to report having a preference for a job that is useful to society (Luechinger et al. 2010).

torate might consequently help to align interests between principals and agents. One effect might be stricter parliamentary oversight, since public servants face lower control costs due to their experience and information advantage. The increased oversight activity induces the government and its subordinate public service to provide public goods and services more efficiently. According to this line of reasoning, public servants as legislators have a positive impact on the execution of sovereign authority, which also includes the reduction of its abuse by means of parliamentary control. A stronger representation of public servants in parliament is thus expected to reduce corruption and also the waste of public funds.

Overall, the net effect of incompatibility rules and the actual representation of public servants in legislative assemblies on political outcomes is theoretically undetermined and invites an empirical investigation.

4.2 Empirical analysis

Following the theoretical reasoning, we analyze the statistical relationship between the representation of public servants in parliament and two broad measures of political outcomes: perceived corruption and government consumption. The indicators are described in Table A.5 in the Appendix. We present different estimation specifications for both outcome measures, including two which are based on an instrumental variable approach.

In Table III.4, we look at the partial correlations between the political selection of public servants as well as the incompatibility rule and the absence of corruption based on an index from Kaufmann et al. (2008). This index synthesizes a rich base of data capturing the phenomenon of corruption. In panel I, we study the partial correlation between a strict incompatibility regime and absence of corruption, controlling for the log of GDP per capita and the Freedom House democracy rating. While no statistically significant correlation for the incompatibility variable is observed, economic development and democracy are related to less perceived corruption.

Panel II emphasizes the partial correlation between the representation of public servants in parliament and the absence of corruption. We find that a larger fraction is related to less corruption. A 10-percentage-points higher fraction of public servants is statistically significantly related to a 0.09 point increase in the index for absence of corruption.

In order to test the robustness of the partial correlation, the estimation in panel III includes the legal origin of a country's legal system and the sum of exports and imports as a percentage of GDP. The latter variable serves as a proxy for the extent of openness to foreign competition. In addition to income per capita and democracy, the legal origins as well as the openness to trade are important predictors in previous work on corruption (see, e.g., La Porta et al. 2008, Treisman 2007, Persson and Tabellini 2005, and Serra 2006). We find that the fraction of public servants in parliament remains statistically significantly associated with less perceived corruption. The coefficients of the control variables are consistent with prior results in empirical research. Together, the factors account for 86.6% of the variation in the dependent variable.

Table III.4
Representation of public servants and absence of corruption
Dependent variable: Kaufmann absence of corruption index

	I	II	III	IV	V
Strict incompatibility or ineligibility	–0.074 (0.12)	–0.006 (0.12)	0.010 (0.12)		
Adjusted fraction of public servants		0.009** (0.4e-3)	0.008* (0.4e-3)	0.010 (0.01)	0.006 (0.02)
Ln(GDP per capita)	0.445*** (0.05)	0.452*** (0.05)	0.414*** (0.05)	0.453*** (0.05)	0.413*** (0.05)
Democracy rating	0.164*** (0.04)	0.173*** (0.04)	0.169*** (0.05)	0.174*** (0.05)	0.168*** (0.05)
UK legal origin			0.318** (0.14)		0.316** (0.14)
German legal origin			0.120 (0.17)		0.116 (0.17)
Scandinavian legal origin			0.688** (0.29)		0.703* (0.37)
Trade (% of GDP)			0.002* (0.00)		0.002 (0.00)
No. of obs.	70	70	66	70	66
R^2	.823	.833	.866	.833	.866
Prob. > F	0.000	0.000	0.000	0.000	0.000

Notes: Panels I to III are OLS estimations. Panels IV and V: Instrumental variable estimator. Results are from the second stage of the two-stage least squares estimator. Standard errors in parentheses. The fraction of public servants is instrumented by the variable capturing a strict incompatibility or an ineligibility regime. The dependent variable is the average score of the Kaufmann corruption index for the years 2003, 2005 and 2007. The reference category in the panels III and IV is "French legal origin".
Significance levels: * $.05 < p < .1$, ** $.01 < p < .05$, *** $p < .01$.
Sources: See Tables A.2–A.5.

While we consider this latter correlation interesting as such, it might well be the result of a causal relationship running from perceived corruption to political selection rather than the direction analyzed in the theoretical part. In particular, candidates from the public sector might get more electoral support in a relatively less corrupt political system. In this constellation, a two-stage estimation approach is recommended in order to further explore the relationship between political selection and corruption. However, we are not aware of an adequate instrument with which to perform our preferred analysis separating the selection from the accountability channel discussed in Section 4.1. Instead, based on the observation that there is no independent correlation between the incompatibility rule and perceived corruption, we take the variable covering a strict incompatibility or an ineligibility regime as an instrument. We do this assuming that there is no direct institutional effect on corruption. The effect is rather indirect. As analyzed in the Sections 2 and 3, the incompatibility regime is theoretically and empirically a strong predictor of the representation of public servants in parliament. In addition, in most countries, the incompatibility of a public service office with a parliamentary mandate is included in the earliest constitutional provisions and can thus be considered a long-standing institution that is basically unrelated to current political outcomes. Panels IV and V report the results of the second stage of the two-stage least squares estimation. If we only exploit the variation in the representation of public servants that is due to the strict incompatibility or the ineligibility regime, we still observe a positive correlation with the absence of corruption with a point estimate of similar magnitude. However, based on the instrumental-variable estimation, it cannot be rejected that there is no effect of the representation of public servants on corruption.

Table III.5 reports the results for general government final consumption as a share of GDP. Current theories of the size of government concentrate on factors affecting the long-run equilibrium of the supply and demand for public goods and services. We take the average over the years 2000 to 2008 in order to smooth out short-run shocks to the supply and demand for public goods. We proceed as before and take some major determinants of government consumption into account. Panel I includes a dummy for strict incompatibility or ineligibility in addition to the log of GDP per capita and the democracy rating. The institutional restriction is negatively correlated with government consumption. Panel II adds the adjusted fraction of public servants. This variable is strongly and statistically significantly positively correlated with government consumption. In countries with a 10 percentage points higher representation of public servants, government consumption is roughly 2 percentage points higher. This correlation holds in panel III if we include four further predictors of the size of government: openness to trade, two demographic variables capturing the fraction of the population under 15 and over 65 years of age, and an indicator of ethnic fractionalization. The four variables have been identified as basic variables in empirical research on government size (see, e.g., Shelton 2007).

Obviously, a larger government also offers a larger pool of political candidates and more voters potentially favouring candidates with a public service background. The partial correlation for the fraction of public servants might thus reflect effects in both directions. Here, we again apply an instrumental variable approach in order to explore the effects of the representation of public servants in parliament. In panels IV and V, we exploit the variation that is due to the variable covering a strict incompatibility or an ineligibility regime. A positive effect is estimated. However, the standard error for the point estimation is too large to draw firm statistical conclusions.

In sum, the phenomenon of a strong representation of public servants in parliament

Table III.5
Representation of public servants and government size
Dependent variable: Government final consumption expenditure (% of GDP)

	I	II	III	IV	V
Strict incompatibility or ineligibility	−1.428 (1.27)	0.231 (1.11)	0.404 (1.13)		
Adjusted fraction of public servants		0.215*** (0.04)	0.230*** (0.04)	0.185 (0.14)	0.176 (0.15)
Ln(GDP per capita)	0.477 (0.51)	0.608 (0.42)	0.160 (0.56)	0.590 (0.42)	0.257 (0.64)
Democracy Rating	0.453 (0.49)	0.657 (0.41)	0.280 (0.45)	0.629 (0.43)	0.255 (0.47)
Trade (% of GDP)			–0.000 (0.01)		–0.001 (0.01)
Population under 15 years (%)			0.069 (0.13)		0.105 (0.16)
Population over 65 years (%)			0.461* (0.24)		0.469* (0.24)
Ethnic fractionalization			–0.158 (2.57)		–0.278 (2.55)
No. of obs.	65	65	62	65	62
R^2	.100	.384	.453	.378	.437
Prob. $> F$	0.091	0.000	0.000	0.027	0.051

Notes: Panels I to III are OLS estimations. Panels IV and V: Instrumental variable estimator. Results are from the second stage of the two-stage least squares estimator. Standard errors in parentheses. The fraction of public servants is instrumented by the variable capturing a strict incompatibility or an ineligibility regime. The dependent variable is the average of the government final consumption expenditure for the years 2000 to 2008.
Significance levels: * $.05 < p < .1$, ** $.01 < p < .05$, *** $p < .01$.
Sources: See Tables A.2–A.5.

is correlated with the absence of corruption and more government consumption in a statistically robust way. However, instrumental variable estimations do not so far allow us to identify causal effects in either direction between the variables.

5 Concluding remarks

In this chapter, we adopt a more person-centered view of the political process. We argue that the individual characteristics of politicians matter for public policy choices and government outcomes. This contrasts with the reasoning of many political philosophers and political economists that good governance is (solely) the result of institutions which allow that politicians are held accountable for their behavior. According to this latter view, it is useless to call for more competent and honest politicians in order to remedy malfunctions such as corrupt behavior.

Obviously, the two views are not mutually exclusive. As political control and the credibility of policy commitments are always limited, a careful selection of representatives is important to bring the outcomes of the political process closer in line with citizens' preferences when delegating decision-making power. We think that a comparative institutional analysis of political selection bridges the two views and emphasizes questions that have been neglected so far in political economics. First, which are the institutions systematically affecting political selection; i.e., the composition of the pool of politicians with regard to identity or quality characteristics? Second, are there consequences for political outcomes stemming from institutions that are primarily set up with the intention of holding politicians accountable? On the one hand, institutions which focus on reducing agency problems might not only tame the potential misbehavior of politicians in office, but also deter some citizens from entering politics in the first place; for instance, those citizens who seek to abuse their political power for private interests. Some outcome observations from the political process that are attributed to accountability mechanisms might thus, in fact, be due to political selection. On the other hand, an emphasis on control mechanisms could also backfire if it systematically changes the pool of candidates for the worse.

The incompatibility of a public sector position with a political mandate is one such institution. It is introduced in various forms to prevent conflicts of interest and thus to reduce agency problems. We have argued that this institution also systematically changes the pool of available candidates and elected politicians because a strict incompatibility regime increases the opportunity costs incurred by public servants when pursuing political mandates. Our main analysis is consistent with this hypothesis. We find in a cross-country analysis based on a novel dataset that, on average, there are 7 percentage points fewer public servants in parliaments in which a strict incompatibility or an ineligibility regime is applied.

In an explorative study on the consequences for political outcomes, the fraction of public servants in parliament was found to be positively related to government consumption and the absence of corruption.

Chapter IV: Theory and Evidence on the Determinants in Germany*

1 Introduction

In order to restrict the abuse of sovereign authority, government functions are assigned to different bodies in a democracy (precept of the separation of powers). Though broadly applied in principle, the concrete personal separation is set differently based on specific institutions in every democracy. A major constitutional decision concerns the degree of compatibility of employment in the public service with election to the legislature. In the United States and in the United Kingdom ineligibility applies; i.e., public servants have to withdraw from office even before they accept a candidacy and have no claim to reemployment in the former position after the election. In contrast, in countries like Austria and Germany there are weak and strong forms of incompatibility, but no ruling of ineligibility exists. In fact, a large proportion of parliamentarians in these countries is from the public service.[1]

Even though the strong representation of public servants in parliaments has raised public concern it has not yet sparked much scientific research. The existence of personal unions and affiliations or the perk of guaranteed reemployment compromise the constitutionally proposed (party-)political neutrality of the public service and generate a conflict of interest. This is due to these parliamentarians' double role as agents in public service and as principals that supervise the public service in parliament. It might be hypothesized that, as a consequence, the public service enjoys substantial discretion, which prejudices the efficient execution of public services. On the contrary, there is a rationale emphasizing that public servants present a reservoir of highly skilled and motivated people who benefit the system in drawing on their specialist knowledge in legislation and monitoring. A strong representation of public servants might then be expected to increase government performance. Independent of these two opposing arguments, it might be said that the electorate has chosen these representatives in the first place. However, citizens can choose among only those fellow citizens who are willing to run for a parliamentary seat and who are supported by a major political party.[2] In

* This chapter is based on joint work with Alois Stutzer. It is a shortened version of the article with the title "Public Servants in Parliament: Theory and Evidence on Its Determinants in Germany", published in *Public Choice*, 145(2-3), 2010, 223-252.

1 For Germany, we include all employees that concurrently hold public law contracts and receive public pay. Public servants elected to parliament generally come from professions in education (i.e., teachers or university professors), the armed forces, the police, public hospitals, the judiciary, various fields of public administration including mayors and district administrators (*Landräte*). Also included are employees of public enterprises. Privatizations are also taken into account; e.g., the major privatizations in the 1990s of Deutsche Post and Deutsche Telekom. With a fraction of public servants in the working population of 13.3% (in 2005), the public service in Germany is relatively large compared to, for instance, the United States or Switzerland.

2 Citizens' choice might be further restricted by electoral rules prescribing closed lists in proportional representation.

order to understand who is selected into parliament, we need to take a step back and study such aspects as the incentives that motivate individuals to opt for a candidacy.

Based on the considerations in the preceding chapter, we rivet on the institutional determinants of the selection of public servants into politics in more detail. We analyze the way in which specific legal provisions offer public servants incentives to pursue a candidacy for a parliamentary mandate and quantify to what extent these affect their representation in the legislature.[3] This is a first step towards better understanding a phenomenon, termed pejoratively in German *"Verbeamtung der Parlamente"* (i.e., parliaments becoming dominated by people with public service status).[4] We develop a general political economics framework and complement it with specific institutional details for Germany and its Laender. The theoretical focus is on issues of incompatibility and a wide set of related institutions that determine in a comparative perspective the cost-benefit calculus of running for a seat in parliament (supply side). In particular, we investigate how, for example, the compensation for holding office in abeyance during parliamentary membership and subsequent automatic promotion affect the attractiveness of a political mandate. Moreover, we look at how aspects like local and temporal availability and specific political human capital favor or adversely affect the chances public servants face in the race for a seat compared to other professional groups. A set of empirically testable hypotheses is derived. The theoretical analysis is expanded with a short discussion of the role of public servants as voters (demand side).

Based on a novel data set, some of the theoretically analyzed determinants are tested empirically. For all the German states, we compiled data on the fraction of public servants in parliament and on the legal restrictions and privileges applied to public servants over the last 60 years. As main results, we find that the granting of compensation for holding office in abeyance is statistically related to a larger fraction of public servants in parliament, whereas the application of a strict as well as a soft incompatibility rule, signifying higher opportunity costs, is correlated with a smaller fraction of public servants in parliament.

In addition to contributing to the literature on political selection our work is related to contributions in administrative science and comparative constitutional law on issues of incompatibility (e.g., van Aaken 2005; von Arnim 2006). Closest to our study in the German context is the careful work by the political scientists Klatt (1976, 1980) and Schrode (1977), who discuss the potential causes and consequences of the representation of public servants in parliaments. However, they neither provide a systematic account of the determinants in one cohesive framework nor do they offer an empirical test on representation.

---

3 Abstracting from differences in the legal status, the terms 'public servant' and 'employee in the public service' (*Beamter* or *Angestellter im öffentlichen Dienst*) will be used interchangeably. Within the German institutional context, the rules of civil service law are similar to those bearing on a large segment of employees in public service. Differences will be mentioned if it is important for the outlined arguments. In the Public Choice literature, the term 'bureaucrat' is often used for the analysis of public sector behavior. Although it is often pejorative in popular usage, the term bureaucrat is used by economists in a descriptive sense and has no inherently derogative connotation (see Tullock 1965 and Niskanen 1971).

4 In Germany, the issue was taken up in some popular books (von Arnim 1991, Scheuch and Scheuch 1992).

Section 2, first, presents the theoretical framework capturing institutional incentives in the selection of public servants as candidates for political offices. Second, the role of public servants as voters is briefly discussed. In Section 3, thc empirical analysis is presented. A detailed description of the compiled database is followed by an econometric analysis of the partial correlations between institutional factors and the fraction of public servants in German Laender parliaments (*Landtage*). Section 4 offers concluding remarks.

2 Theoretical considerations

The conditions under which public servants are allowed to sit in the legislature and their situation once they are in it shape incentives to run for a seat and are reflected in the fraction of public servants in parliament. We briefly mention the basic trade-off between the separation of powers and political representation that is relevant in the decision on ineligibility and incompatibility of a position in the public service with a parliamentary mandate. Pursuing a rational choice perspective, a detailed benefit and cost calculus is discussed based on the specific institutional details in the German Laender (Section 2.2). The analysis is complemented with some thoughts on public servants as voters (Section 2.3).

2.1 Ineligibility and incompatibility of public service with a parliamentary mandate

Institutions governing the personal separation of powers in a democracy affect the basic trade-off between issues of agency and selection. Stricter personal separation not only reduces agency problems arising from the intrapersonal conflicts of interest but also limits the pool from which competent and honest people can be selected for a specific mandate. The more public servants are barred from taking up parliamentary mandates, the more difficult it is for citizens to elect candidates who have a high degree of expertise in public service issues and the necessary information to effectively monitor the government and its subordinate public service. The latter is important in order to attenuate the situation of asymmetric information between the legislator and the bureaucracy as emphasized in the work by Niskanen (1971). Whether public servants as legislators in fact care about the preferences of citizens and use their discretion accordingly depends on their motivations and the kind of incentives that can be applied to hold them accountable for their decisions.

(Intra-personal) interlinkages of interests and the attractiveness of a parliamentary mandate are most curtailed when public servants are not eligible to stand for parliamentary election and even have to resign before accepting a candidacy. Ex-public servants may still feel an obligation towards public service but their interlinkages are reduced to informal ties. Much weaker restrictions constitute rules of incompatibility. With strict incompatibility, public servants have to hold their office in abeyance but may remain in office until they are elected for a mandate; they often have guaranteed reemployment subsequent to the termination of their mandate. With soft incompatibility, only some categories of public servants are restricted, whereas all other public servants can continue in their public service career, often with a guaranteed reduced work load.

2.2 The cost-benefit calculus of running for political office

The process of selecting public servants as legislators can be divided into at least three stages that are linked by institutions and the strategic considerations of the agents involved.[5] In a first stage, the focus is on what motivates a public servant's decision to run for office. In our main analysis, we examine the cost-benefit calculus of a public servant to predict his or her entry decision. In the second stage, citizens decide for whom to vote for. We only touch upon this aspect in Section 2.3. The third stage concerns elected politicians' policy decisions. The latter includes the discretion of a mandate and feeds back to the attractiveness of a candidacy. A public servant is expected to run for office if this activity offers the highest expected utility among his or her available alternatives. In order to avoid being too abstract, we discuss the cost-benefit calculus regarding the specific legal provisions holding for the German Laender.

We have two comments at the outset. First, there are, of course, differences in initial incentives to run for a seat in parliament depending on the branch and position in the public sector. Some public servants might value, e.g., the expected gain in status and discretion and the utility derived from the position. Others might be driven more by ideology and various motives of rent extraction. However, the focus of our contribution is less on these differences than on the institutional factors that are expected to provide incentives that affect the cost-benefit calculus of public servants in the same direction (when they consider running as candidates for a political mandate). Second, our analysis is conceived as being comparative. With additional privileges for public servants, a political mandate becomes relatively more attractive for them and relatively less attractive for potential candidates from all other sectors.[6]

Pecuniary compensation for the political mandate

The compensation of politicians is an important policy variable in an economic model of political selection (e.g., Besley 2004) and gets particular attention in empirical research on the benefits (and costs) of holding office (e.g., Di Tella and Fisman 2004). Depending on the specific institutions, compensation here includes the income from the mandate, fringe benefits, the lump-sum reimbursement of costs incurred in exercising the mandate (*Aufwandspauschale*) and the right to a pension as the main material benefits. In the German context, and specifically for public servants, there is an additional compensation for having to hold one's office in abeyance while sitting in parliament. These different forms of benefits will be discussed in turn.

5 The three-step analysis follows the theoretical literature in the tradition of the so-called citizen-candidate model (see Besley and Coate 1997 as well as Osborne and Slivinski 1996).

6 It would be interesting to analyze more systematically the cost-benefit calculus for such other people, in particular for lobbyists (sponsored by trade unions, professional associations or large firms). Unfortunately, we have no specific institution in our newly generated data set that directly addresses variation in the attractiveness of a political mandate to lobbyists.

Base compensation. For a member of a parliament in the German Laender the base compensation is between 4,000 and 6,200 euros per month in 2007. City states have the lowest base compensation. In addition, there are a number of fringe benefits that are rather non-transparent. Whether the package for legislators is attractive to public servants, based on a simple compensation comparison, will depend on their individual position in the salary and career scale, as well as their tenure. Senior public servants in a ministry or mayors in bigger cities earn more in public service than they would from the scheduled compensation allocated to parliamentarians. This is different for public servants in the middle and even some upper grades of the civil service, like administrative officers, teachers, as well as mayors in smaller cities. The relative financial attractiveness of a mandate holds all the more strongly after the increase in parliamentary allowances (*Diäten*) following the decision of the German constitutional court in 1975 (BVerfGE 40, 296 [296]).

Privileges involving pension benefits, tenure, promotion and benefit offsetting. Many specific provisions enacted for public servants sitting in Laender parliaments were based on the law covering the legal status (*Rechtsstellungsgesetz*) of the members of the public service elected to the federal parliament. The latter was derived mainly from civil service salary law, civil service career law, as well as public services law. While there is substantial variation in these provisions across the Laender (that we exploit in our statistical analysis), we describe some of them here to illustrate the issues involved.

First, when the Laender started introducing pensions for parliamentarians (around 1970), a calculation of claims was chosen that was advantageous to members with public service backgrounds; i.e., the years (incompatible) public servants spent in parliament were counted twice.[7] The years were taken into account once in determining the pension entitlements from the mandate, and once again for the public service pension scheme. In the latter case, pension claims were accumulated although no services were rendered.

Second, the law in some Laender counted fully the years during which a political mandate was held for the tenure in public office (*Besoldungsdienstalter*), which is the most relevant factor for determining a public servant's basic salary.

Third, in Bavaria and Bremen for some years, incompatible public servants were automatically promoted when they resumed their public service duties, as if they had been holding office in an exemplary manner.

Fourth, it was prohibited to offset income (pay or pension) from a public office against the parliamentary allowance or the parliamentary pension.

All four institutional provisions constitute particular benefits to public servants and render an elective office in parliament more attractive. Employees of large firms or representatives of trade unions or professional associations may encounter similar or even more advantageous conditions, but they have no legal claims, depend on the discretion

7 The requirements for a parliamentarian to be entitled to an old-age pension are usually a minimum age (between 55 and 65) as well as a minimum membership of six to ten years. The pension is, in most cases, at least 35% of the base allowance and increases for each additional full year that a mandate is execised by around 3% of the allowance but to no more than 70% in total (Braun et al. 2002: 207).

of their superiors and may be bound to a direct equivalent in terms of interest representation.

In 1975, the German constitutional court declared these four promotive provisions to be unconstitutional and not in conformity with civil service law principles. The federal as well as the Laender parliaments had to respond to this ruling by reforming the legal status of public servants elected to parliament. As a result, the years that public servants had spent in parliament could no longer be taken into account in the civil service pension scheme, and the provision of an automatic promotion has been suspended as well. In all Laender now, only 50% of the years spent in parliament are counted toward tenure in office. Moreover, parliamentary allowances and old-age pensions above a certain amount have to be offset against income (salary or pension) from the public office.

Abeyance compensation. A specific additional pecuniary benefit to public servants that increases the attractiveness of a political mandate is the compensation for having to hold one's office in abeyance (*Ruhegehalt*). Based on Article 137 of the German constitution, many public servants have to leave their office vacant for the time they accept a mandate. Abeyance pay was introduced as a compensation for this ban on holding office.[8] Exceptions were the part-time parliament in Hamburg and the senate in Berlin. Public servants in these parliaments are put on leave without payments (Klatt 1976: 47-50). Abeyance compensation amounted to between 35% and 75% of the allowable salary (*ruhegehaltsfähige Dienstbezüge*) and was increased automatically after every legislative period (Dietrich 1976: 97). A further subtle, but financially attractive, benefit for public servants (but not for other employees of the public service) was the ongoing receipt of abeyance compensation after the termination of the mandate until commencement of the old-age pension (von Arnim 1980). Public servants were able to resume their former office (or a comparable office in terms of pay) upon their own request. However, the awarding of a decent abeyance compensation created incentives to retire early. Following the decision of the German constitutional court in 1975, public servants have to request reemployment within three to six months after the termination of the mandate if they do not want to lose this claim. Furthermore, they generally face stricter requirements with respect to the resumption of their public office (Braun et al. 2002).

In contrast, when taking up a mandate employees in the private sector have no legal claim to (partial) continuation of payments if they stop working for their employer.

Finally, there is the possibility of earning a secondary income (e.g., honorariums from speeches, employment by a foundation or a mandate in an international organization or some supervisory board). For public servants, this possibility is restricted when holding an office in public service but attractive when holding a mandate and put on leave; in particular, if the mandate is not very time-consuming. According to data from the 11th and 12th legislative period of the Landtag of North Rhine-Westphalia, roughly one-

8 This was based on the law on the legal status of members of the public service elected to the German parliament of August 4, 1953 (BGBl. I p. 777). Given that an abeyance compensation is a payment for the public servant without fulfilling any public office duties, the abeyance compensation has never been in conformity with civil service law principles (Braun et al. 2002).

fifth of public servants exercising a mandate generated additional income outside the parliamentary arena (Holthoff-Pförtner 2000: 85).

In sum, we hypothesize that these specific privileges make a parliamentary mandate relatively more attractive and increase the fraction of public servants in the parliaments of the German Laender.

Opportunity costs of a political mandate

Whether a mandate is attractive for a potential candidate depends not only on the compensation but also on his or her opportunity costs; i.e., the lost income from an alternative occupational engagement as well as the loss in disposable time. For public servants, a mandate involves lower opportunity costs if it is legally compatible with their job in the public service. Independent of the profession, there are lower opportunity costs of time with a part-time parliament. However, as will be explained below, a parliament will differentially effect the attractiveness of a mandate when studied in interaction with other institutions depending on whether it has a part- or full-time organization.

A crucial but difficult issue is how a mandate depreciates or appreciates a person's human and social capital. For instance, one might query whether the opportunity costs of a mandate are generally positively correlated with marketable professional skills in the private sector (Gagliarducci et al. 2010). The advantages of gaining prominent status and contacts with a mandate might well be more valuable to a highly-skilled, private-sector person both while in office and even more so subsequent to it. Between sectors, a mandate might be relatively more attractive for public servants as their job-specific human capital is closer to government activity and thus less likely to depreciate.[9] Specific administrative knowledge as well as familiarity with legal issues facilitate the meeting of legislatory requirements and decrease the costs of holding a mandate.

Moreover, public servants might be more available (time, location) than employees in other sectors or self-employed people (with the exception of professional politicians). In addition, at the local level head officers, mayors and district administrators may be better known to the public than other professionals. Both, greater availability and publicity reduce public servants' costs of campaigning.

Incompatibility. In the German Laender, there are three different arrangements defining the compatibility between a position in public service and a political mandate:[10] (i)

9 However, for representatives of professional associations, trade unions or for members of parliaments that receive a second income from large firms, social capital might also not depreciate and even increase with their additional insights into the political decision process and with their enhanced reputation.

10 At the federal level, the Parliamentary Council, entrusted with the formulation of the German constitution (*Grundgesetz*), established Article 137 in 1949, which authorized all levels of jurisdictions to impose incompatibility rules on public servants. Following the pressure of the occupying powers, the Parliamentary Council enacted an electoral law comprising strict incompatibility for the first federal elections. This law also included a guaranteed reemployment for all public servants running for the federal parliament. Mayors and district administrators being the only exemption; i.e., they were not subject to an incompatibility rule and had no guaranteed reemployment. The strict rule of incompatibility was absorbed in the first law on the legal status (*Rechtsstellungsgesetz*) of the members of the public service elected to the lower house of the German parliament (*Bundestag*) in 1951 (see Bundesgesetzblatt (BGBl.) I p. 297). A compensation for holding office in abeyance (*Ruhegehalt*) was added in 1953 (see BGBl. I p. 777).

compatibility, (ii) soft incompatibility restricted to specific positions in the public service (or alternatively defined in terms of specific compatible positions), and (iii) strict incompatibility involving employment in the public sector in general. While strict incompatibility increases the opportunity costs for all public servants, soft incompatibility increases them only for some public servants. Depending on the Land, certain public servants (e.g., senior government officials, magistrates, prosecutors and mayors) as well as public servants employed on the same federal level as their parliamentary office (i.e., public servants at the Laender level) are incompatible with a mandate in the Laender parliament.

Full-time parliament. The organization of a parliament in being either a part or full-time regime will largely determine the work schedule and time commitments of a mandate and the amount of time a parliamentarian has at his or her disposal. In the German Laender, there are full-time parliaments except for Baden-Württemberg (till 2011), Berlin, Bremen and Hamburg. However, the transition from a part-time to a full-time parliament is not officially defined. We refer to specific legal provisions for identifying full-time parliaments. For many Laender, the introduction of the law on the members of parliament (*Abgeordnetengesetz*) following the decision of the German constitutional court in 1975 can be considered as initiating full-time parliamentarism. This law comprised often noticeably higher allowances, which were subject to income taxation for the first time, higher reimbursements for costs incurred in exercising the mandate, a right to an assistant, disability-, health- and survivor insurance, as well as an end of service equivalent. Considering public servants who have offices compatible with a mandate, a part-time parliament involves lower opportunity costs because they are still able to partly fulfill their job in the public service. However, this also holds for other candidates. It might even be argued that a part-time parliament is particularly attractive to professional and self-employed individuals because they can still carry on some business or maintain major client contacts. In the situation where public servants are incompatible with a mandate, a full-time parliament is more attractive than a part-time parliament because the former pays its members a higher compensation for the mandate. Moreover, the status of the parliament also affects the extent to which a mandate depreciates a person's human and social capital. With a full-time parliament, self-employed people and other professionals are at a disadvantage compared to incompatible public servants who can spend more time on their parliamentary duties and on campaigning for reelection.

Employment guarantee. Opportunity costs in terms of reduced employability after a mandate are substantially reduced for public servants but not for candidates from other sectors. Public servants have a legal claim on resuming their former office (or a comparable office in terms of pay) after they resign from parliament or are not reelected. Other professions also enjoy dismissal protection granted by the principle of the independent mandate and incorporated in Article 2 of the law on members of parliament. However,

Since the law for the members of the federal parliament (*Bundesabgeordnetengesetz*) entered into force in 1977, which extended the incompatibility to mayors and district administrators but abolished the compensation for holding office in abeyance, no major changes have taken place. For a detailed description of the historical evolution and a comparative constitutional law discussion of the incompatibility rule see Tsatsos (1970).

the dismissal protection holds only for one year following the termination of a mandate and can be suspended, given there is some "serious" reason (Braun et al. 2002: 60). The guaranteed and detailed legal right to reemployment for public servants provides them with a long-term advantage which increases their institutionally granted independence and reduces the risks associated with a political career. Another case in point is that former public servants retiring from their parliamentary mandate are regularly observed to pursue a career in the private sector (revolving door phenomenon). In fact, a political mandate might be particularly attractive to public servants who would like to leave the public service. On the one hand, a political mandate does not compromise a position held in the public service as it is guaranteed. On the other hand, a political mandate allows side jobs that were not possible while working for the public service. These jobs provide an ideal starting position for entering the private sector.[11]

Campaign leave. A peculiarity in earlier German civil service law was the entitlement of candidates to up to two months leave for the purpose of preparing the election campaign (*Wahlvorbereitungsurlaub*), notably with full compensation. This privilege reduced the opportunity costs of public servants when running for a seat, a project not easily juggled with a career. The Laender (with the exception of Berlin) introduced this opportunity for paid leave based on German constitutional law (Article 48) and abolished it following the decision of the German constitutional court in 1975.

In sum, we predict that soft and, even more so, strict incompatibility reduces the attractiveness of a political mandate for public servants. However, if a parliament is operated as a full-time organization rather than a part-time one, the effects of the incompatibility restrictions are expected to be (at least partly) offset. This compensating effect is expected to be larger for strict incompatibility than for soft incompatibility.[12] Moreover, we expect that the reemployment guarantee as well as the remunerated campaign leave increase the fraction of public servants in parliament.

2.3 Public servants as voters

So far, we have mainly discussed the institutional provisions promoting the supply of public servants as parliamentary candidates. In this section, we look at a complementary aspect in outlining the *demand* for public servants as legislators. We emphasize the role of public servants as voters, often organized in public trade unions, and analyze the attractiveness of public servants as candidates for political parties.

The bureau voting model of government growth hypothesizes that public servants are more likely to cast their votes in elections. This model assumes that public servants

11 Moreover, a political mandate is often the last feasible possibility for climbing the career ladder (even though it is, of course, not within the same hierarchy but in a related institution). Examples are senior teachers (*Oberstudienrat*), head teachers (*Schulrektor*), lord high commissioners (*Oberkommissar*) or mayors.

12 As argued above, in a regime where public servants are compatible, no unambiguous hypothesis can be formulated with regard to the organization of the parliament as part- or full-time and its relative attractiveness for public servants. In our sample of German Laender, we do not observe the association of compatibility with a full-time parliament and can therefore not empirically study the net effect.

hold marked political opinions and therefore favor candidates advocating higher government spending (Garand et al. 1991). The high turnout of public servants has been documented in several studies (see, e.g., Bush and Denzau 1977, Frey and Pommerehne 1982, Moe 2006). In their research, the higher turnout rates for public servants compared to employees from other sectors are partly explained by characteristics specific to them as a group: on-average higher levels of education; greater union membership; and higher satisfaction and trust levels in the way democracy works. In addition, greater interest in politics is identified. This might be ascribed to their occupational interest as well as the lower costs of acquiring relevant information (Corey and Garand 2002). Concerning policy preferences, it has been shown that teachers tend to vote for more expenses on education (Frey and Pommerehne 1982) and public servants in general tend to favor center-left parties (Garand et al. 1991).

Public sector unions not only mobilize public servants as voters but also try to coordinate their voting behavior in favor of candidates who implement union-member interests (Moe 2006). As no binding policy commitments are possible, public sector unions concentrate on their selection of candidates. In this way, public servants are likely to support their policy interests, either owing to professional identity or because they are personally positively affected by the union's preferred policies. This strategy is sustained when public servants vote for their peers, expecting similar policy preferences.

Public servants are also attractive candidates for political parties in general. While holding a political mandate, senior officials and mayors may use public service facilities to execute their parliamentary duties. This allows the party to reduce expenses by passing mandate-related work on to the public service. Given the time flexibility of public servants on (partial) leave while holding a mandate, parties are more likely to recruit them for a political career that requires them to tread the mill of innumerable mandates (*"Ochsentour"*). In Germany, for example, public servants were also eligible for up to two-months-paid leave in order to prepare the election campaign. This possibility was abused by parties. They nominated public servants for unwinnable positions on the party lists in order to get publicly subsidized campaign workers (Klatt 1980: 32). Given public servants' right to reemployment, the party does not have to care about a public servant's professional future on resigning or not being reelected.

However, the institutional provisions or office-related advantages render the public servant elected to parliament relatively independent of party leaders and party obligations. As a result, parties have to trade off the attractive characteristics of public servant candidates against the lower bargaining power they have once they hold office.

3 Empirical analysis

3.1 Data

The empirical analysis is based on a newly compiled dataset for the fraction of public servants in all the parliaments of the German Laender or city states as well as the specific legal provisions defining the attractiveness of a political mandate for public servants. Currently, there are 16 German states or Laender. Up to the German reunification, there were 11 states, the so-called old German Laender. The empirical analysis covers the time period after the Second World War. Accordingly, the longitudinal data covers a period spanning between 62 years (Bavaria) and at least 14 years in the new German Laender.

Composition of parliaments in the German Laender (*Landtage*)

There is some literature in political science studying the occupational composition of the German Laender parliaments (see, e.g., Hess 1976; Holl 1989; and Handschell 2002). Mostly for single election periods, statistics were published in the journal entitled *Zeitschrift für Parlamentsfragen*. The main data sources are, however, the parliamentary handbooks (*Volkshandbücher*), which are published for every election period. They ideally contain information about the occupational composition of the parliament or, otherwise at least, sufficient information about the occupations held prior to entering parliament in short curricula vitae for the individual parliamentarians. Based on the latter information, we were able to code occupations and determine the professional composition (i.e., the fraction of members of parliament with a public service background). For example, the occupational composition of the 15th Bavarian legislature (2003-08) indicates that 70 representatives or 38.8% of the members of parliament were recruited from the public service. Of these 70 members, 19 were employees within public service and 51 had the status of public servants. They had previously held the following functions: educational professions (40%), administration (32.8%), judiciary (10%), municipal officials (10%), mayors (4.3%) and police and armed forces (2.9%).[13] The remaining representatives' backgrounds were self-employment (i.e., lawyers, entrepreneurs or farmers/cultivators) (41.1%), employment in the private sector or in professional associations (15.5%), housekeeping (2.3%) and others (2.3%). A complete list of the data sources for the dependent variable is provided in Table B.1 in the Appendix.

Overall, there is information about the fraction of public servants in parliament for 177 legislative periods.[14] There is no information for some early legislative periods

13 For some countries, a higher proportion of members of parliament with a public sector background among left parties is reported by Blais et al. (1997). It might thus be expected that their representation in parliament correlates with the fraction of seats won by the center-left parties. However, in Germany many mayors, district administrators, and senior public servants elected to parliament are affiliated with the Christian Democratic Union (CDU). As a consequence, there is no systematic difference to the Social Democratic Party (SPD). For the Free Democratic Party (FDP), a lower level of public servants within their faction is observable. However the trend is towards a larger fraction. For the remaining smaller German parties (e.g., the Greens), there is no systematic pattern (Schindler 1999). In sum, no clear party-specific hypothesis with regards to the selection of public servants into parliament can be derived.

14 Regular terms last either four or five years. Due to constructive votes of no confidence and coalition instabilities, some legislative periods turned out to be shorter.
For 114 legislative periods, we could adopt the fraction of public servants in parliament from sources that offer aggregate information on the composition of parliaments (see Table B.1 in the Appendix). For another 14 legislative periods, we adjusted aggregate data for the category 'members and former members of the government' based on entries for single members of parliament. For these 128 legislative periods in total, the subcategorization of public servants elected to parliament varies strongly. In several Laender and years, there is no further categorization. In other Laender (and, in particular, in more recent years), there are separate categories for members of parliament that are from the judicial branch, the administration

Figure IV.1
Fractions of public servants elected to the Laender parliaments of North Rhine-Westphalia, Baden-Württemberg and Bavaria between 1946 and 2008

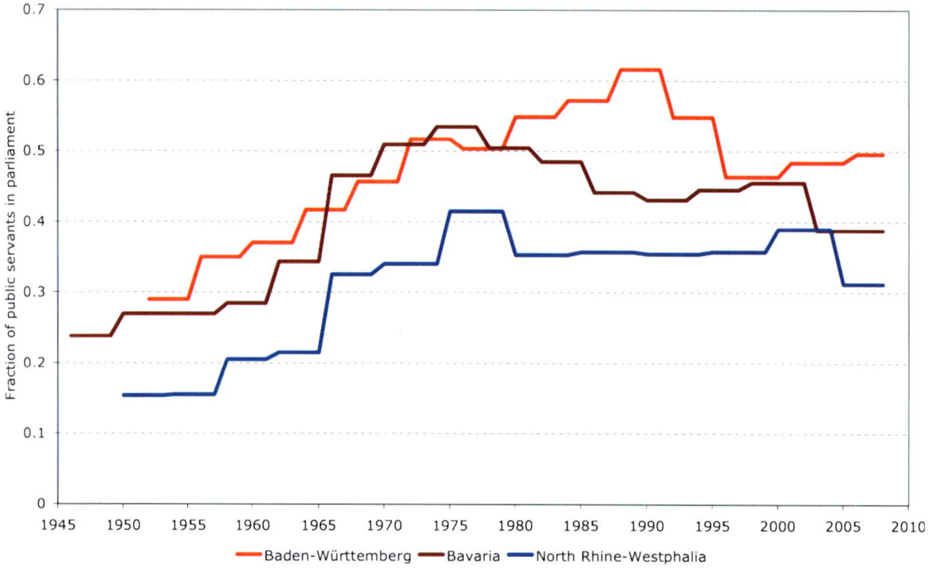

Sources: Official parliamentary handbook series of the Laender parliaments (see also Table B.1 in the Appendix).

due to data unavailability and data incomparability (see the last paragraph of this subsection). On average, the fraction of public servants in our sample is 39.6%; it was lowest in Lower Saxony in 1947 (10.6%) and highest in Baden-Württemberg in 1988 (61.6%). The descriptive statistics for each of the Laender are presented in Table B.2 in the Appendix.

Figure IV.1 traces the fraction of public servants in parliament over time for the three largest Laender; i.e., North Rhine-Westphalia, Baden-Württemberg and Bavaria. The fraction in all the three Laender increases until the mid-1970s. In Baden-Württemberg and in Bavaria, the fraction reached a level above 50%. While the level in North Rhine-Westphalia has been rather stable around 40% since the early-1980s, there has been

or the education sector. Besides, there are some parliamentary information services that group their members of parliament according to rank or federal level. Finally, for some Laender, there is a change in the usage of subcategories over time. Accordingly, we abstained from a differentiated data collection and generated aggregate data on the fraction of public servants. For the remaining 49 legislative periods, we coded individual level information from single entries in parliamentary handbooks.

about a 10-percentage point decline in Bavaria until the mid-1990s and a second peak in Baden-Württemberg around 1990.

In collecting and compiling the data on the fractions of public servants in parliament, we encountered several theoretical and methodological challenges. First, existing statistics on the socio-economic composition of parliaments differ in their intended purpose. In contrast to our study, which concentrates on the last occupation before being elected to parliament, some studies focus on educational background, the occupation learned (Handschell 2002), gender or race (Norris 1997, Norris and Lovenduski 1995). As a consequence, the distinction between the last occupation and the occupation learned often causes ambiguities. Second, for early legislative periods, occupational statistics either do not exist or are of poor quality because they are based on voluntary self-disclosure. Moreover, the way categories were defined sometimes changes within a time series causing structural breaks. As far as we observed such changes, we coded the members of parliament in question on the basis of their entries in the parliamentary handbooks. However, analyzing individual curricula vitae raises problems (mostly for early periods) in terms of unclear chronologies of apportionments. For the current analysis, we restrict our sample to legislative periods for which we were able to compile reliable data.

Institutional conditions for public servants as members of parliament

A series of different laws include provisions that define relevant claims of public servants who either run for office or have a mandate. These are the law on the members of parliament (*Abgeordnetengesetz*) and its precursors (*Gesetz über die Rechtsstellung der Abgeordneten* or *Diätengesetz*), the civil service law, the electoral law and the incompatibility law. For some points of time, surveys for specific provisions in all the Laender were published in the journals entitled *Zeitschrift für Parlamentsfragen* and *Zeitschrift für Beamtenrecht*, in the series *Recht und Organisation der Parlamente*, and in a few law dissertations (Sturm 1967 and Tsatsos 1970).

We coded information for seven important institutional characteristics relevant for public servants.[15] All the institutional variables are coded as dummy variables.

- *Strict incompatibility:* Strict incompatibility is given and coded 1 (0 otherwise) if all the public servants have to hold their office in abeyance while in parliament. The reference category captures compatibility; i.e., public servants elected to parliament do not face any incompatibility restrictions.

  Soft incompatibility: Soft incompatibility is given and coded 1 (0 otherwise) if only some specific categories of public servants have to hold their office in abeyance while in parliament. The reference category is again compatibility.

15 There are, of course, additional factors that are relevant for the attractiveness of a mandate such as its remuneration. However, these factors apply to all the candidates. A specific benefit for public servants is their legal claim to reemployment after they resign from parliament. This entitlement has not been changed since the Laender parliaments were constituted. Accordingly, the effect of this factor on the relative attractiveness of a mandate for public servants cannot be isolated in our statistical analysis.

- *Full-time parliament:* Laender parliaments are coded as either full-time parliaments (1) or part-time parliaments (0). As there are no Laender that simultaneously had a full-time parliament and compatibility, the correlation between full-time parliament and the fraction of public servants in parliament cannot be calculated ceteris paribus. Instead, we can only estimate the interaction effect in the two incompatibility regimes. Therefore, two interaction terms (taking the value 1) are included: one for "strict incompatibility x full-time parliament" and one for "soft incompatibility x full-time parliament".
- *Pension benefit:* If for pension entitlements of public servants the years in parliament are counted twice (i.e., not only for the pension from the mandate but also for the pension from the service in the administration), a pension benefit is given and coded 1 (0 otherwise).
- *Abeyance compensation:* If extra compensation for holding one's office in abeyance is granted, the variable takes value 1 (0 otherwise).
- *Automatic promotion:* The variable takes value 1 (0 otherwise) if public servants are automatically promoted when they reenter office.
- *Other privileges:* This variable integrates four factors that grant preferential treatment to public servants in parliament and that were abandoned following the decision of the German constitutional court in 1975. These factors are: (i) guaranteed two-month paid leave to prepare the election campaign, (ii) prohibition on offsetting income (pay or pension) from a public office against the parliamentary allowance or the parliamentary pension, (iii) right to continuation of payments of the compensation for holding office in abeyance after resigning from the mandate and until entry into the old-age pension or until a reappointment was requested by the public servant or imposed by the public employer (employees of the public service had no claim to this provision), and (iv) complete accounting of the years with a mandate for the tenure in office. Only if three of these four factors apply, substantial privileges are in place and the variable takes value 1 (0 otherwise).

Table B.3 in the Appendix gives an overview of the institutional conditions holding in each state over time, and Table B.4 in the Appendix reports their relative frequency in the data set. Five parliaments introduced a strong incompatibility ruling when they were constituted after the Second World War (Lower Saxony and North Rhine-Westphalia) or after the German reunification (Saxony-Anhalt, Brandenburg and Thuringia). Two Laender abolished compatibility and adopted strict incompatibility (Bavaria 1970 and Bremen 1967). Other Laender introduced a soft incompatibility and replaced it by a strict incompatibility rule in the 1970s (e.g., Saar, Rhineland-Palatinate and Hesse). Baden-Württemberg (until 2011), Berlin and Hamburg as well as the new Laender, Saxony and Mecklenburg-Lower Pomerania, still impose soft incompatibility on public servants.

Pension benefits due to double allowance for the years in parliament were granted for a relatively short time in most Laender; i.e., mainly between the late-1960s and the late-1970s with the exception of Hamburg and Berlin where this double allowance never applied. The compensation for holding one's office in abeyance was offered for some time in all the old Laender, except in the city states Hamburg and Berlin. Bavaria was the last Land to introduce it in 1970 and also one of the first to abandon it again in 1978 (together with Lower Saxony and Hesse). While the federal constitutional court declared this provision to be unconstitutional, some Laender simply labeled it differently and set an upper limit on it. Abeyance compensation (now called compensation amount, *Ausgleichsbetrag*) is still offered in Baden-Württemberg and Bremen.

All parliaments in the old German Laender started as part-time parliaments. Only four part-time parliaments now remain (Baden-Württemberg, Bremen, Berlin and Hamburg). All new German Laender started with full-time parliaments.

Automatic promotion only applied for a few legislative periods in Bavaria (1970-77) and Bremen (1967-1978). The specific privileges that we integrate in one variable, and that were criticized in the decision of the federal constitutional court in 1975, were introduced in almost all the Laender between 1950 and 1963 (Bavaria 1970 and Bremen 1967 being the exceptions) and abandoned in revisions of the law between 1977 and 1980.

For all institutional conditions studied in our analysis, there is no variation in the new German Laender over time. Accordingly, we cannot use observations for the fraction of public servants in these Laender parliaments to identify the quantitative effect of the different legal provisions when we take Laender-specific effects into account at the same time.

Regarding the collection of the institutional variables, some challenges had to be met. First, many provisions were laid down in the laws on the legal status of public servants elected to parliament. However, other relevant provisions had to be found in the civil service law, the electoral law or some other regulations. Second, in order to establish a chronological order of the provisions in force (especially for the early periods), specific commission protocols, plenary debate protocols and specific bills (law proposals and drafts) had to be studied. In light of the difficult political and institutional circumstances in the late 1940s and early 1950s in some Laender, no corresponding provisions had been introduced.

3.2 Results

The empirical analysis focuses on the partial correlations from multiple regressions between the institutional conditions for public servants as members of parliaments and their actual representation in them. We report the results for a series of estimation specifications in order to uncover as much information as possible about our data pool. Accordingly, the institutional effects are identified under different assumptions about unobserved factors in our time-series, cross-section data.

The first set of results is based on the full sample, including observations from the old and the new German Laender. Panel I in Table IV.1 reports the results of a pooled OLS estimation. Partial correlations for eight institutional variables are estimated. It is found that strict incompatibility is related to a smaller share of public servants in a part-time parliament (the reference regime being "compatibility x part-time parliament")[16], while pension benefits, abeyance compensation and automatic promotion are related to a larger share. The existence of a full-time parliament offsets the negative effect of strict incompatibility on the representation of public servants. The set of other privileges summarized in a separate variable is related to a lower fraction of public servants in parliament, counter to our hypothesis. Together the factors account for 40.2% of the variation in the dependent variable, and the F-test indicates that the explanatory variables are jointly statistically significant. With regard to the size of coefficients, e.g., in Laender and years with strict incompatibility, on average, the fraction of public servants in part-time parliaments is 13.4 percentage points lower than in part-time parliaments where a mandate is compatible with a position in the public service ceteris paribus.

However, results from pooled estimations might be biased due to omitted variables. On the one hand, there might be socio-economic or institutional conditions in some Laender that are not captured by our variables but that systematically affect the attractiveness of political mandates for public servants (and are not orthogonal to our institutional variables). On the other hand, there might be unmeasured time-specific effects on the representation of public servants in the legislature that are correlated with some of the institutional variables. A factor mentioned in our theoretical framework is public servants as voters. As there exists no comparable data on public-sector employment over the time range of our study, this determinant cannot be included directly. Instead, we take unobserved Laender and time-specific variation into account, including Laender-fixed effects (panel II), decade-fixed effects (panel III), or both (panel IV) in our specifications.

The changes in the estimated partial correlations and the statistically significant Laender and decade effects indicate that the effects of our institutional variables cannot easily be separated from unobserved Laender characteristics and time effects.[17] The partial correlations show that strict incompatibility is related to a sizeably smaller fraction of public servants in part-time parliaments (between -12.4 and -17.5 percentage points) independent of the inclusion of the fixed effects. With Laender and/or time-fixed effects there is also a negative correlation (between -7.0 and -10.2 percentage points) for soft incompatibility. The negative effect of strict incompatibility is estimated to be systematically lower in Laender with a full-time parliament. A less clear picture emerges for soft incompatibility in Laender with a full-time parliament. In specification IV, no compensatory effect is measured.[18] The variable capturing pension benefits has a small positive effect (around two percentage points, not statistically significant) on the fraction

16 As there are no observations for Laender that simultaneously assume compatibility and maintain a full-time parliament, the pure effect of adopting a full-time parliament cannot be estimated. Instead, the effect for full-time parliament is always conditional on having an incompatibility regime. Accordingly, the effects for the variables full-time parliament are formulated as interaction terms. It follows that the coefficients for the two incompatibility variables (interpreted alone) hold for part-time parliaments.

17 With regard to explanatory power, the inclusion of Laender-fixed effects alone shows an R^2 of 32.6%. In comparison, the R^2 in panel II including the explanatory variables and Laender-fixed effects is 45.6%.

18 The finding is in line with the theoretical reasoning in Section 2.2 that the compensation effect of a full-time parliament is smaller in a soft incompatibility regime than in a strict incompatibility regime and that the net effect is inconclusive.

Table IV.1
Determinants of the representation of public servants in German Laender parliaments
Basic estimations for all Laender
Dependent variable: Fraction of public servants in parliament

	I	II	III	IV
Strict incompatibility	–0.134***	–0.124***	–0.175***	–0.125***
	(0.033)	(0.034)	(0.032)	(0.029)
Soft incompatibility	0.008	–0.102***	–0.070**	–0.094***
	(0.029)	(0.038)	(0.033)	(0.031)
Strict inc. x full-time	0.195***	0.199***	0.146***	0.069**
parliament	(0.024)	(0.025)	(0.025)	(0.029)
Soft inc. x full-time	0.043*	0.073*	0.036	–0.020
parliament	(0.025)	(0.041)	(0.023)	(0.037)
Pension benefit	0.099***	0.105***	0.022	0.026
	(0.023)	(0.020)	(0.026)	(0.023)
Abeyance compensation	0.138***	0.130***	0.126***	0.044*
	(0.021)	(0.024)	(0.019)	(0.023)
Automatic promotion	0.126***	0.127***	0.050	0.069*
	(0.042)	(0.040)	(0.039)	(0.036)
Other privileges	–0.105***	–0.082***	–0.065**	–0.050**
	(0.021)	(0.022)	(0.027)	(0.024)
Laender fixed effects	No	Yes	No	Yes
Decade fixed effects	No	No	Yes	Yes
Prob. > *F*	0.000	0.000	0.000	0.000
R^2	0.402	0.456	0.560	0.660
N	177	177	177	177

Notes: Partial correlations from OLS regressions. Standard errors in parentheses. Significance levels: * $.05 < p < .1$, ** $.01 < p < .05$, *** $p < .01$.
Sources: Data compiled based on the sources listed in Tables B.1 and B.3 in the Appendix.

of public servants in parliament once time effects are taken into account. For abeyance compensation a positive effect is estimated that is around four percentage points in specification IV with the complete set of fixed effects. The estimated effects of automatic promotion are also positive. The inclusion of fixed effects reduces the size of the effect. The effect of the variable capturing other privileges is negative, rather than positive as hypothesized, and amounts to -5 percentage points in the fourth specification. Overall, the choice of specification matters for the size of the estimated coefficients (but less so for the direction of the estimated correlations). Due to this sensitivity, we explore the data with additional specifications.

In Table IV.2, we concentrate on the independence of observations in our sample. This is done based on the observations from the old German Laender, as with Laender-fixed effects: observations from the new German Laender do not contribute to the identification of the effects of the institutional variables. Estimations in Table IV.1 are based on the assumption that all the unexplained parts of the fraction of public servants in parliament (i.e., the residuals) are independent across space and time. However, there are many reasons why a positive residual for a specific legislative term is positively correlated with the residual of the next term. In particular, due to the electoral advantage of incumbent members of parliament,[19] positive and negative "shocks" to the fraction of public servants in parliament carry over to the subsequent terms. The average length of stay in German parliaments is about two to two-and-a-half periods (see, e.g., Holl 1989 and Mielke and Reutter 2004). In fact, an inspection of the residuals shows significant autocorrelation. We take this aspect of the political process into account by including the lagged dependent variable in our specification.[20] As lagged dependent variables are often used instead of time-fixed effects, we estimate one specification without decade effects (panel II) and one with decade effects (panel III). In order to allow a comparison with a specification not including the lagged dependent variable, panel I reports estimation results with Laender and time-fixed effects for the old German Laender. For the specifications including the lagged dependent variable, we calculate panel corrected standard errors taking into account panel heteroscedasticity. This is recommended judging from the differential variation of the residuals across Laender.[21]

The following empirical findings emerge from these refined estimations. As theoretically expected from the incumbency effect, the past level of public servants in parliament systematically and substantially affects the current level. According to specification III, a 10-percentage point increase in the past legislative term is related to a 5.1 percentage points higher fraction in the current legislature. Consistent with the hypothesis regarding opportunity costs, strict incompatibility is related to a substantially smaller fraction of public servants in Laender with a part-time parliament, an effect that is robust across specifications in Tables IV.1 and IV.2. It seems that this effect is smaller in full-time parliaments. However, the size of the offsetting effect is not precisely measured. The negative effect of soft incompatibility is smaller than for strict compatibility in part-time parliaments. No effect of compensation is measured once the lagged dependent variable is taken into account. The theoretical predictions for the effect of various (pecuniary compensation) benefits on the selection of public servants are not rejected. Pension benefits, abeyance compensation and automatic promotion all are positively correlated with the fraction of public servants in parliament. The largest coefficient is estimated for abeyance compensation, statistically significant at the 10% level. When public servants receive compensation for holding their office in abeyance, their representation in parlia-

19 For a theoretical account of the incumbency advantage see, e.g., Ferejohn (1977).

20 We follow Beck and Katz (1995) and give this specification priority over a time series approach specifying an AR(1).

21 We started based on the assumption of homogeneity as our dependent variable takes values between 0 and 1. However, an analysis of residuals across Laender indicates Laender-specific (or panel) heteroscedasticity.

Table IV.2
Determinants of the representation of public servants in German Laender parliaments
Extended estimations for the old Laender
Dependent variable: Fraction of public servants in parliament

	I	II	III
Lagged fraction		0.690***	0.511***
of public servants		(0.076)	(0.084)
Strict incompatibility	–0.125***	–0.119***	–0.123***
	(0.029)	(0.033)	(0.030)
Soft incompatibility	–0.094***	–0.096***	–0.096***
	(0.032)	(0.036)	(0.033)
Strict inc. x full-time	0.069**	0.063***	0.035
parliament	(0.029)	(0.022)	(0.023)
Soft inc. x full-time	–0.020	0.014	–0.019
parliament	(0.037)	(0.034)	(0.034)
Pension benefit	0.026	0.051***	0.016
	(0.023)	(0.016)	(0.020)
Abeyance compensation	0.044*	0.063***	0.033*
	(0.023)	(0.020)	(0.020)
Automatic promotion	0.069*	0.044	0.021
	(0.036)	(0.037)	(0.033)
Other privileges	–0.050**	–0.020	–0.006
	(0.024)	(0.019)	(0.022)
Laender fixed effects	Yes	Yes	Yes
Decade fixed effects	Yes	No	Yes
Prob. $> F/Chi^2$	0.000	0.000	0.000
R^2	0.677	0.791	0.829
N	156	145	145

Notes: Partial correlations from OLS regressions. Panel-corrected standard errors for estimations II and III taking into account panel heteroscedasticity. Significance levels: * $.05 < p < .1$, ** $.01 < p < .05$, *** $p < .01$.
Sources: Data compiled based on the sources listed in Tables B.1 and B.3 in the Appendix.

ment is 3.3 percentage points higher on average ceteris paribus (specification III). The variable capturing other privileges is no longer related to the fraction of public servants in parliament if the full set of controls and the lagged dependent variable are taken into account.

In sum, the empirical findings are in line with the predicted effects for the institutional variables. In particular, the major restriction of strict incompatibility and the main privilege of abeyance compensation are statistically systematically related to the fraction of public servants in parliament.

4 Concluding remarks

The separation of powers and a responsible government are major principles in a democracy that are sustained by a set of checks and balances. However, the implementation of these principles in a set of (formal and informal) institutions is solved differently in various democracies around the world. This situation has called for comparative institutional research to be carried out in order to identify the government structures that are most conducive to a political process that fulfills citizens' preferences. So far, most of this research has focused on the allocation of decision-making power between legal entities (i.e., the *functional* separation of powers). However, there is also the *personal* separation of powers (i.e., the idea that individual people are not selected for multiple offices). This selection might be (legally) strict or operate through incentives for self-selection to different offices.

In this chapter, we laid out an analytical framework based on a cost-benefit calculus to explore the selection of public servants into legislatures. In our empirical analysis for the German Laender based on a novel data set, we find that in many Laender and for many of the years a substantial fraction of the parliamentary mandates was represented by members of the public service. In fact, in 17.5% of the legislative terms more than half of the mandates went to public servants. In 50.8% of the terms at least 40% of the elected politicians had a public service background. Moreover, we find that institutional restrictions in terms of incompatibility rules substantially reduce the selection of public servants into Laender parliaments. On the other hand, the privileges granted to public servants when pursuing a political career, in particular compensation for holding one's office in abeyance, increase the fraction of public servants in parliament. An important privilege for public servants is also that of guaranteed reemployment subsequent to resignation from parliament or non-reelection. However, this advantage in the political process could not be quantified as it holds throughout time and Laender. Based on our analysis, we think that the economic approach is well suited to account for the fraction of public servants in parliaments and that it can be productively applied to other specific institutional environments.

There are several avenues for further research and further discussions following our study and findings. First, the observation of a large fraction of public servants in Laender parliaments could be discussed from a political representation perspective (e.g., Mansbridge 2003, Pitkin 1967, Schwartz 1988). There is an obvious disproportionality in representation with respect to professional background (a dimension of *descriptive* representation following the categorization of Pitkin 1967). Accordingly, (work) life experiences of the representatives are expected to be systematically different from those of the represented. For instance, experiences on how to survive in the private market are represented less. Second, there is the question of *substantive* representation. To what extent do the elected politicians with a public service background represent and serve the interest of their constituents? The strong representation of public servants in the legislature is expected to systematically affect the political process, e.g., with regard to the parliamentary oversight of government activity and the outcomes of the political process. Of particular interest are consequences for allocative efficiency of the public sector as well as its productivity. Third, based on a better understanding of the selection effects of specific features of democratic institutions, it should become possible to understand policy outcomes as being more the result of political selection or more the result of holding politicians accountable.

Chapter V: Consequences for Legislative Oversight*

1 Introduction

The oversight of the government and the subordinate public service is one of the constitutional core duties of the members of parliament in a democracy. It is a key aspect of the checks and balances in a system adhering to the principle of the separation of powers. Parliamentary oversight is instituted to restrict the abuse of government authority and to maintain incentives to efficiently provide public goods and services. Even though economists and political scientists alike emphasize the importance of legislative oversight to hold governments accountable, it is more often than not abstracted from the actual parliamentary control process in scientific work.[1]

In this chapter, we intend to contribute to a better understanding of the parliamentary oversight process in three directions. First, we explicitly study the use of parliamentary control instruments. Second, we consider parliamentary control as the result of political selection and of the institutional structure determining political competition. Third, with regard to political selection, we focus on the role of public servants as legislators in parliamentary control. We understand political selection as the process and the result of any systematic effect of institutions on the composition of political bodies. As to parliamentary control, political selection affects the composition of the legislature in terms of its members' individual control costs and individual motivation. The two aspects are difficult to separate though. The cost of control efforts can be lower due to skills, knowledge, an information advantage or a specific motivation to control (e.g., due to public service motivation or civic duty, etc.).

We argue that the selection of public servants into legislatures is of particular interest for understanding how political selection affects parliamentary oversight. First, parliaments across the world differ widely in the fraction of (former) public servants in their compositional structure. In the United States or the United Kingdom, there are relatively few former public servants in the national parliament as they are ineligible to run for a seat. In contrast, in the legislatures of Denmark, Austria or Germany, for example, the share of public servants has often reached more than forty percent since World War II. Second, public servants might systematically differ in terms of their individual cost and motivation for parliamentary control. On the one hand, the selection of public servants to the legislature can serve as a check. If the information asymmetry between the public service and the legislature is severe (as, e.g., pointed out by Niskanen 1971), electing insiders to parliament who become accountable to the electorate might help to align interests between principals and agents. Public servants in parliament who dispose of an

* This chapter is based on joint work with Alois Stutzer. It is the basis for the article with the title "Political Selection of Public Servants and Parliamentary Oversight", published in *Economics of Governance*, 14(1), 2013, pp. 45–76.

1 For our purpose, we use the terms of parliamentary control, oversight, and monitoring interchangeably. For descriptions of oversight see, e.g., Rosenthal (1981) and Patzelt (2005).

information advantage with respect to public service issues and who face lower control costs enhance the monitoring competence of the elected assemblies. On the other hand, public servants in parliament compromise the principle of the (personal) separation of powers and thus face a conflict of interest. This is due to their double role as agents in public service and as principals that supervise the public service in parliament. In sum, it is an open question whether the specific motivation and individual control costs of public servants in parliament lead to more or less parliamentary oversight for a given level of political competition. The focus of our analysis refers to this latter question.

In addition, we lay out a general framework of parliamentary oversight based on the dispersed literature on this issue. This provides a theoretical rationale for a set of further determinants taken into account in the empirical analysis. While we mainly treat them as control variables, we consider them interesting as such.

We empirically study parliamentary oversight for the institutional context of Germany and its sixteen Laender. We do this for mainly two reasons: First, parliamentary control of the government and its subordinate public service is a main task of the members of parliament in the German Laender. Most new law is enacted on the federal level while the Laender have to implement and administer it. Second, members of parliament with a public sector background are a striking feature of politics in Germany.

With respect to the instruments of parliamentary control, we focus on the most widespread instruments; i.e., major and minor interpellations and oral inquiries.[2] By asking for detailed information and evaluations with regard to the efficient use of public funds, interpellations critically control government behavior. Information about the use of these control instruments is publicly available, subject to media attention, and individually attributable. Thus, it is relevant for constituents' evaluations of a politician's performance. We take the use of these instruments to be positively related to the strictness of parliamentary oversight.

For the empirical analysis, a unique time-series, cross-sectional data set has been compiled covering three different quantitative measures of parliamentary control, spanning the period from 1946 to 2009. Additionally, we gathered data on the fraction of public servants elected to parliament and collected information on the form of government, the electoral system, the margin of victory in electoral races, the number of parties, the seat share of the Social Democrats, and the length of legislative periods.

We find a positive correlation between the political selection variable; i.e., the fraction of public servants in parliament, and the number of parliamentary inquiries submitted. This holds in particular for minor interpellations; i.e., the main individual control instrument for efficiency control. The result is confirmed if we apply an instrumental variable approach instrumenting the fraction of public servants in parliament with its institutional determinants. In addition, we find a generally positive level effect of a mixed-member electoral system on the number of parliamentary inquiries. In mixed-member electoral systems a fraction of the legislature is elected through a majoritarian procedure (rather

2 Depending on the legal framework and the period analyzed, preference may be given to either the term inquiry or the term interpellation. Since the economic interpretation in our context is the same, we abstract from such differences in terminology and rather use the terms interchangeably.

than through a proportional procedure). A majoritarian procedure is understood to increase political competition as *individual* candidates can be held accountable by the electorate.

This study contributes to the research on political selection and on the comparative institutional analysis of parliamentary control. For the former aspect see Chapter II. As to parliamentary oversight, it is related to the (often US-specific) analysis of oversight relationships and bargaining processes between the bureaucracy and the legislator (Banks and Weingast 1992, Calvert et al. 1989, Moe 1989, Niskanen 1971, 1975, Ogul and Rockman 1990, Rosenthal 1981, Weingast and Moran 1983), the (legislative) design of administrative procedures and ex ante control (Bawn 1995, 1997 and McCubbins et al. 1987), and the separation of powers (Persson et al. 1997, Grossman and Helpman 2008). Our analysis also contributes to the limited body of research on the effectiveness of legislators (Grant and Kelly 2008, Padro i Miguel and Snyder 2006 and Shiller 1995), and the German political science literature dealing with state legislatures and governmental-parliamentary relationships (Holtmann and Patzelt 2004, Patzelt 2005).

Section 2 presents the main theoretical arguments about the incentives for parliamentary control with a focus on public servants elected to parliament. The arguments are complemented with a brief discussion on further relevant determinants of parliamentary oversight. Section 3 deals with the German institutional background. In Section 4, the data set and the econometric analysis are presented. Section 5 offers concluding remarks.

2 Theoretical considerations

The institutional structure shapes the incentives of the members of parliament to execute parliamentary oversight. Differences in motivations and skills influence their ability and individual costs to effectively control the executive bodies. In this section, we, first, briefly explain the importance of parliamentary oversight for the democratic process. Second, we discuss politicians' incentives, trade-offs and individual costs when deciding about resources to invest in parliamentary control. This framework is, third, extended to the case of parliamentarians with a public service background. We consider occupational background as an important determinant of economic interests and control costs. Fourth, we take into account additional factors affecting parliamentary oversight.

2.1 Relevance of parliamentary oversight

A major constitutional principle in a democracy is the separation of powers sustained by a set of checks and balances. One primary check that falls within the responsibility of the legislature is the control of the government on behalf of the citizens. The oversight function implies first and foremost the prevention, the detection and the restriction of discretionary executive abuse. Second, oversight is meant to ensure that policies announced by the government and authorized by parliament are properly implemented. This involves an efficiency control. Finally, oversight involves the critical examination of government proposals. This is often referred to as political control with respect to the (partisan) direction in which policies are developed. Overall, there is the idea that strict parliamentary oversight ensures a responsive government and thus an efficient provision of services by the subordinate public agencies.

2.2 Incentives for parliamentary oversight

There are several arguments why legislators have at best moderate incentives to strictly control government behavior despite their constitutional mandate. First, strict oversight has a strong public good dimension within the legislature. Monitoring benefits the whole population and rarely favors single districts or narrowly targeted groups so that it would become individually attractive (e.g., Weingast 1984). Second, monitoring is largely ineffective because the public ministerial administration has a clear informational advantage regarding the costs of producing public services (Niskanen 1971). In particular, the lack of organizational structure and staff resources (Rosenthal 1981) as well as the longer time horizon of public ministerial agencies create a situation where the administration dominates parliament rather than being seriously supervised by it. Moreover, parliamentary attention tends to be sporadic and is often motivated by some scandal calling for control only subsequent to the event (Weingast 1984).

However, there are also incentives encouraging parliamentary oversight. This is taken as self-evident in the literature on the congressional dominance model (e.g., Banks 1989, Calvert et al. 1989, and Ferejohn and Krehbiel 1987). Politicians can spend time on campaigning, legislating, services to district constituents, earning outside income and oversight. For politicians with the relevant political expertise, oversight is an activity that helps them to distinguish themselves from other politicians in the competition for votes. Oversight expertise is acquired during a political career and in previous or current professions. (Aggressive) monitoring is further stimulated by media coverage since it is pursued to attract public attention and to increase one's reputation. Stricter oversight is also expected if the (local) constituency complains about the public provision of goods and services. Constituents reduce the information costs of monitoring by reporting to their representatives. This is particularly relevant if there are well organized interest groups in the politician's district that have sufficient resources and strong incentives to keep a watchful eye on public service behavior (Banks and Weingast 1992).

Several of the previous arguments hint at the role of political competition in shaping the individual politician's cost-benefit calculus. If competitive pressure is stronger, politicians are expected to engage more often in oversight activities.

It is self-evident that the different arguments are more or less relevant for individual politicians in shaping their incentives to engage in parliamentary oversight. There are individual differences in the cost-benefit calculus. Political selection emphasizes this heterogeneity in the pool of people pursuing a political mandate. Politicians are expected to react in a systematically different way to a given level of political competition depending on their individual characteristics. With regard to parliamentary oversight, the individual control costs are of particular importance. Legislators with better knowledge about the functioning of the public service and better access to information about the provision of public goods and public services have relatively lower costs for engaging in parliamentary control.

2.3 Public servants as legislators

Public servants in comparison to legislators from the private sector represent a selection of people in parliament who differ in their incentives, costs and maybe even in their intrinsic motivation for engaging in parliamentary control.

Cost advantage in parliamentary oversight

Information asymmetries between the public service and the legislature are an obstacle to parliamentary oversight. Electing public servants with a high degree of expertise in public service issues to parliament is expected to attenuate this situation. A first informational advantage in public service issues consists of specific knowledge about the proper execution of a public servant's (previous) function. A second component refers to knowledge about the general functioning of the public service as a whole. This involves familiarity with the efficiency control executed by the public employer and ultimately by the parliament. It also includes knowledge about the legal status of public servants; i.e., civil service salary law, civil service career law, and public services law as well as legal and administrative procedures in general. Representatives with a public service background can thus execute parliamentary control at comparatively lower costs. Accordingly, engaging in oversight is relatively attractive for them to promote their reputation and thus to finally win votes. For example, a parliamentarian with a public service background is more receptive to his or her constituents' complaints about the behavior of (local) public agencies. An informational advantage, first, ensures that the costs of becoming informed about local public service nuisances are relatively low. Second, the costs of bringing an issue to parliament by means of parliamentary control instruments (e.g., interpellations) are relatively low, as well. If a public servant in parliament does not plan to return to public service, but intends to pursue a political career until retirement, monitoring becomes an attractive activity for advancement. A final argument refers to fiduciary duty. It states that a career in public service partially reflects public service motivation (Frank and Lewis 2004, Le Grand 2003). If such motivation carries over to behavior in political office, it contributes to a continuous monitoring of government behavior.

Conflict of interest in parliamentary oversight

Public servants face a conflict of interest due to their double role in public service and in parliament. This compromises the personal separation of powers. A large proportion of public servants in parliament may be interpreted as embodying a strong and direct representation of public service interests. As a consequence, the public service enjoys more discretion, which prejudices the efficient provision of public services. The private interests of public servants lead to slack that is less forcefully counteracted by legislative control when the latter is pursued by committees that largely consist of public servants.[3] This conflict of interest counteracts the cost advantage in monitoring.

However, other conflicts of interest might be weaker. Public servants in parliament often enjoy guaranteed reemployment and favorable terms for leave of absence with respect to time and pay. These institutional privileges render them relatively more independent of special interests. Other parliamentarians (e.g., employees of large firms, representatives of trade unions or professional associations and secretaries of parties) may encounter similar or even more favorable conditions while holding a mandate. However, they have no legal rights to reclaim the conditions; they depend on the discretion of their (former) superiors and may be bound to a direct equivalent in terms of interest representation. In contrast to other members of parliament, public servants can be considered relatively independent from outside pressure and free to dedicate themselves to parliamentary duties until the end of their political mandate.

2.4 Additional determinants of parliamentary oversight

Electoral systems and individual accountability

A majority voting system and a mixed-member electoral system, where at least some members of parliament are elected on single seats, provide incentives for individual politicians to distinguish themselves from other parliamentarians or potential competitors and to build up their reputation as dutiful members of parliament. Accordingly, more frequent use of parliamentary control instruments is expected relative to a pure proportional electoral system. This argument concentrates on electoral accountability in a politician's district. However, politicians are also faced with electoral accountability in their party and/or their supporting interest groups. Under proportional representation the latter forces might be stronger than in a majority voting system, e.g., due to the importance of a high rank on the party list in order to win a parliamentary seat. Thus, whether a candidate runs in a marginal (single-member) district or at a marginal rank of its party list, she or he faces increased electoral accountability. Which electoral system, overall, creates stronger incentives for parliamentary oversight is an additional issue. For our hypothesis, we follow the work by Persson and Tabelllini (2005) arguing that politicians in a majority voting system, on average, face stricter electoral accountability.

Political Parties

Parties and their parliamentary representation, the factions, often have a constitutional duty to monitor and actively criticize government behavior. Compared to individual legislators, parties have a longer time horizon (Alesina and Spear 1988). This enhances their interest in sustained oversight activity. Party leaders provide internal rewards and sanctions to induce individual members of parliament to engage in oversight (Niskanen 1975). Moreover, (large) parties can specialize internally (Snyder and Ting 2002)

3 However, it might be argued that a coordinated behavior of public servants in parliament is difficult to implement given the heterogeneity of public servants with respect to party affiliation, branch, function and position within the public service.

to organize parliamentary control and accumulate monitoring specific human capital. Whether or not parties are formally allowed to initiate parliamentary instruments, they can strategically coordinate the use of these individual tools to put pressure on the executive body.

The extend to which parties engage in parliamentary oversight is affected by the degree of party competition. The closer electoral races are expected to be, the stronger are the incentives to engage in oversight.

Related arguments refer to the new parties and the number of parties in parliament and their role in oversight. First, new parties have to distinguish themselves from the other parties and need to become known (Kalke and Raschke 2004). Second, new parties are often elected because of dissatisfaction with the government or with the parties in power. For both reasons, parliamentarians from new parties are expected to use more parliamentary control instruments to actively control government behavior.

Furthermore, the number of parties might reflect the diversity of social interests represented in parliament. More diversity might be another force that enhances the execution of oversight. However, the free rider problem in parliamentary oversight is also more severe with a larger number of parties (as there is less possibility to attribute political failures to individual actors and parties).

One might finally conjecture that the ideological composition of parliaments is related to the engagement in parliamentary control. For example, anti-etatists might mainly care about law reforms to curb public transfers and much less about active oversight to achieve proper functioning of the government. Anticipating the empirical analysis below, this aspect creates a statistical problem if a systematic relationship between the ideological and the professional composition of parliaments exists. So it is often reported that the fraction of public servants is higher in the center-left parties.[4] We take this into account statistically by including information on the party composition of parliament.

Form of government

Parliamentary democracies experience minority governments and governments that are formed by a single party, a coalition or even a coalition of major parties. These different constellations give rise to a large set of strategic considerations when deciding about parliamentary control activity. It is argued that members of the majority party or coalition parties have little incentive to effectively control their own governmental representatives. According to this argument, the larger the majority or the coalition is, the less frequently parliamentary control instruments are used. However, the constituency of the governing majority, for the most part, holds its representatives responsible for the provision of public goods, who thus have an incentive to control the efficient provision of public services and to use the respective instruments.

It might further be argued that parties in opposition have stronger incentives to execute monitoring when they can distinguish themselves from a large fraction of representa-

4 For the German federal parliament, see Deutsch and Schüttemeyer (2003), Kintz (2006, 2010), and Schindler (1999) who report a higher share of public servants in the Social Democratic Party (SPD).

tives; e.g., in situations with coalitions of major parties. Moreover, within coalitions of major parties, oversight incentives might be strengthened as these coalitions cover a large ideological spectrum. Since such constellations are not considered to be permanent, major parties want to signal their independence by controlling the government, respectively the government representatives of the coalition partner. Summing up, no clear theoretical prediction is possible about how any one form of government is related to the overall level of parliamentary oversight.

Other factors
Some use of parliamentary oversight instruments must be seen as an expression of parliamentary activism (see, e.g., Andeweg and Irwin 1993) not intended to control the government. Factors driving parliamentary activism are not investigated any further but are assumed to contribute to the general level of the use of control instruments. Level effects are also expected from the size of the legislature and the length of the legislative periods. In larger legislatures more people are involved in parliamentary oversight, and this is expected to increase the overall use of parliamentary control instruments (overcompensating any free-rider incentive). Similarly, a longer legislative period with more parliamentary sessions, offer more possibilities for parliamentary oversight. Parliaments entrusted with designing the constitution and establishing the most fundamental institutions might concentrate on legislating. The necessary implementation of new law might, however, also provoke more parliamentary oversight.

2.5 Hypotheses on parliamentary oversight

In order to summarize the main arguments and to prepare for the empirical analysis, the key hypotheses are formulated:

Hypothesis 1: The lower the individual costs of parliamentary control are, the more frequently instruments of oversight (given the level of political competition) will be used. Public servants in parliament are identified as legislators with lower control costs; in particular, due to their public sector-specific information advantage. Accordingly, in legislatures with a larger proportion of public servants, there is more parliamentary oversight.

Hypothesis 2: The more parliamentarians are personally held accountable due to electoral restraints, the more effort they invest in parliamentary oversight. A mixed-member electoral system is identified as one where more legislators face the competition of single-member districts than in pure proportional representation. Accordingly, members of a legislature who are selected under a mixed-member system make, on average, more frequent use of instruments of parliamentary oversight.

Furthermore, for legislatures where electoral races have been more contested, we subsequently expect more oversight. In legislatures with at least one new party, also a more frequent use of instruments of parliamentary control is predicted. No specific hypotheses are formulated for the number of parties, the party composition of parliaments, constitutional parliaments and the form of government as parliamentarians face countervailing incentives to engage in oversight.

3 Institutional background

The theoretical arguments are studied for public servants elected to German Laender parliaments. In Germany, the core competencies of the Laender mostly concern public service issues, such as education, cultural affairs, administrative law, police law, and municipal law. An important competence is also the actual formation of the implementation rules of federal laws (*Ausführungsbestimmungen*). The latter aspect implies that most sovereign duties are executed by the public service of the Laender or local authorities. Both of these are subject to the supervision of Laender parliaments. In fact, most of the time and resources of the parliamentary process at the Laender level (and significantly more than at the federal level) are devoted to controlling government behavior rather than to legislating (Patzelt 2006).

Parliamentarians in the German Laender have access to different instruments to pursue their oversight mandate in order to hold the government accountable. The major means for obtaining information and controlling government and public-service behavior are the power to pass the budget (*Budgethoheit*), the institution of committees of inquiry and parliamentary interpellation rights.[5] Some of these instruments are stipulated in the constitution. More commonly, they are part of the rules that govern parliamentary procedures.

We focus on the parliamentary instruments of inquiry or interpellation. Parliamentary inquiries oblige the executive body to provide the information or explanation requested (Article 20, paragraph 2, of the German constitution). This includes access to documentations, unsolicited assistance, ministerial reports, and written comments. In addition, government declarations have to accommodate parliamentary control matters (Reutter 2008).[6]

The German parliaments generally allow three types of parliamentary inquiry: major and minor interpellations and oral inquiries. Box C.1 in the Appendix provides procedural details for their application. Major and minor interpellations focus on the effective use of public funds. While major interpellations address issues of broader coverage and contain questions reaching from constitutional concerns to government's intentions regarding possible reforms, minor interpellations aim at narrower issues. They form the classical tool for efficiency control. Parliamentarians use interpellations to collect information and to demand explanations, justifications and assessments of the conditions that prevail in the various fields of public service activity. Moreover, interpellations often deal with the impact of reforms and demand the government to thoroughly clarify its stance on the measures taken. Apart from questions that critically examine executive behavior, interpellations also include questions aiming at governments' intended policy actions. Typical areas of concern are the judiciary, the police, education, infrastructure,

5 Further institutions to control government behavior include the right to demand the attendance of members of the government (*Ministerzitierung*), public auditing institutions (*Rechnungshöfe*), specialized offices of ombudspersons (e.g., the commissioner for the armed forces), petition committees, and the judicial review (*Normenkontrollklage*) before the German constitutional court. For an overview of the German institutional framework, see Schindler (1999). For a comparative survey on oversight instruments in national parliaments see Yamamoto (2007).

6 For a discussion of parliamentary interpellation instruments, see Russo and Wiberg (2010).

and the public administration. Oral inquiries are also submitted in order to collect information and demand explanations. However, they often address current issues and matters related to news events. An example for a minor interpellation is presented in Box C.2 in the Appendix.

In sum, procedural rules force governments to react. They serve as a threat of launching a debate or transforming an interpellation into an interpellation of higher order thereby steering media attention. All aspects affirm the role of interpellations as strong parliamentary oversight devices.

4 Empirical analysis

4.1 Data

The empirical analysis is based on a newly collected dataset on the use of parliamentary control instruments in all the parliaments of the German Laender and city states as well as on the factors influencing parliamentary oversight. The empirical analysis covers the time period since the late 1940s (with a maximum of 63 years for Bavaria and a minimum of twelve years for the new German Laender).

Parliamentary instruments of inquiry

Data on the aggregate use of interpellations and inquiries is collected from various sources. For some Laender and some time periods, descriptive studies in political science offer data.[7] Additional information is from parliamentary handbooks (*Volkshandbücher*) and from the parliamentary online documentation systems of the Laender. They provide detailed information for recent legislative periods. In order to collect information on early legislative periods, we analyze parliamentary printed matter or protocols as well as government declarations. These materials were provided by the parliamentary information services.

For the three instruments, i.e. major and minor interpellations and the oral inquiries, there is information for 152, 153 and 133 legislative periods respectively. There is no information for some early legislative periods due to data availability. Some Laender introduced oral inquiries only in later periods. We take this into account in the empirical analysis as oral inquiries are likely to have replaced some minor interpellations.

Descriptive statistics for each of the instruments is presented in Table C.1 in the Appendix. On average, the number of major interpellations submitted within a legislative period is 66.6. For minor interpellations, the average number is 1663.6, and for oral inquiries, the respective number is 545.9.

Figure V.1 illustrates the number of minor interpellations submitted in all the German Laender parliaments over time. No systematic pattern is observed; neither over time nor across Laender.

7 In particular, we draw on Kalke and Raschke (2004), Mielke and Reutter (2004), Raschke and Kalke (1994), Reutter (2008), and Schäfer (2005).

Figure V.1
Use of minor interpellations in German Laender parliaments

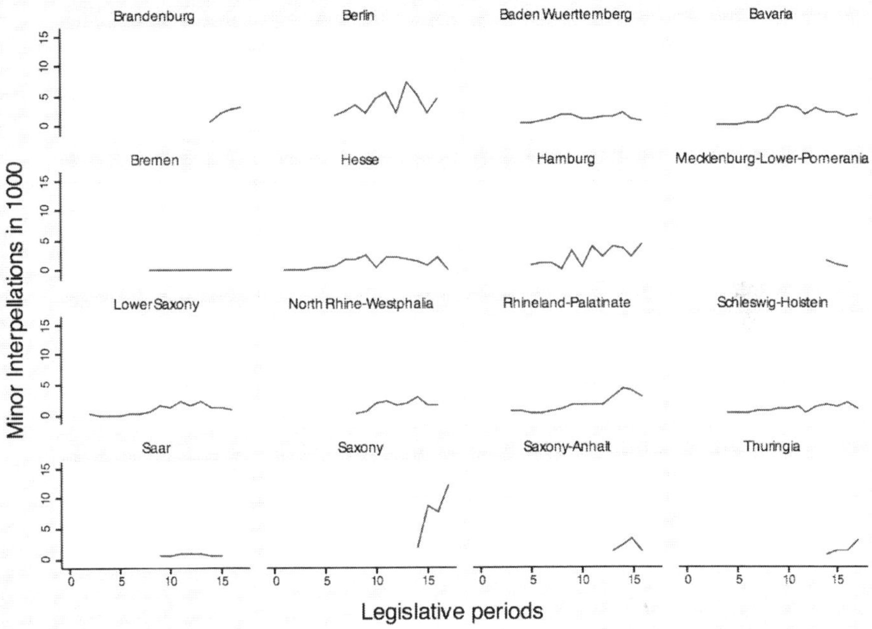

Note: The legislative periods are numbered backwards in order to obtain comparable time-series. The 17th legislative period always stands for the latest legislative period.
Sources: See Table C.1.

In collecting the data on the three instruments for parliamentary inquiries, we encountered some challenges. In some cases, contradictory information about the number of submitted inquiries exists. The number of minor interpellations and oral inquiries varies because some researchers and officials count only the number of inquiries that have received replies. In some sources, it is not taken into account that inquiries not replied to in time can be transformed into higher order interpellations and that an unexpected termination of a legislative period may cause unanswered inquiries. As far as we noticed such ambiguities, we clarified the observations in question with the help of the parliamentary information services.

Explanatory factors

In the empirical analysis, we take into account a large set of factors that are theoretically related to parliamentary oversight. We describe the explanatory variables for the largest sample; i.e., for minor interpellations.

- *Fraction of public servants*: This variable captures the percentage of parliamentarians with a previous or concurrent occupation in the public service.[8]

  Mixed-member electoral system: This variable for the electoral system (based on Massicotte 2003) is coded 1 (0 otherwise) if some candidates are directly elected while others enter via a party list.[9] The reference category is a strictly proportional electoral system. In 2010, 14 Laender apply a mixed-member electoral system. Within our sample period, three Laender have switched from a strictly proportional electoral system to one with a majoritarian component. No switches in the other direction have been observed. The relative frequency of a mixed-member electoral system in the data set is 73.9%.

- *Margin of victory*: Party competition is approximated by the difference in vote shares between the strongest party and the closest competitor. The average margin of victory is 11.8%.

- *New party*: If at least one new party enters parliament in a legislative period, the variable takes value 1 (0 otherwise). This is the case for roughly one third of the legislative periods in our sample.

- *Number of parties*: This variable states the number of parties elected to each legislative periode. The average number is 3.7.

- *Seat share of the SPD*: The party composition of parliaments is captured by the seat share of the Social Democratic Party in each legislative period.

- *Coalition government by major parties*: The variable for the form of government (based on Manow and Wettengel 2006) takes value 1 (0 otherwise) if the government is supported by a coalition of the major parties (CDU, Christian Democratic Party and SPD, Social Democratic Party). In 14.4% of the legislative periods, the government was composed of the two major parties.

- *Constitutional parliament*: Constitutional parliament is given and coded 1 (0 otherwise) if the parliament is entrusted with designing the constitution.

- *Oral inquiries exercisable*: If the instrument of oral inquiry is introduced separately and is exercisable, the variable takes value 1 (0 otherwise).

- *Legislative period shorter than 1.5 years*: If the legislative period turns out to be shorter than 1.5 years, the variable takes value 1 (0 otherwise).

---

8 See Chapter IV Section 3 for a description of the representation of public servants in German subnational parliaments.

9 In most Laender with a mixed member electoral system, each voter has two votes, a first vote and a second vote. The first vote is directly attributed to a candidate that represents the electoral district. The candidate that obtains the majority of first votes in the districts is elected to parliament by a direct mandate. This is the majority voting component in the electoral system. With the second vote, the citizens vote for the party which may then, in accordance with its share of party votes, send candidates from closed party lists to parliament. This is the proportional voting component in the electoral system. For a detailed description of the electoral system including the discussion of bonus seats (*Überhangmandate*), compensatory additional list seats (*Ausgleichsmandate*) and further differences between the Laender, see Massicotte (2003).

- *Legislative period between 1.5 and 3 years*: The variable takes the value 1 (0 otherwise) if the legislative period turns out to last between 1.5 years and 3 years.
- *Legislative period regular 5 years*: If the regular legislative period lasts 5 years, the variable takes value 1 (0 otherwise).

4.2 Results

The results are presented in several steps. We start with an overview of the partial correlations between the identified determinants and the three parliamentary control instruments. Subsequently, we focus our analysis on minor interpellations. Our theoretical considerations fit the use of this instrument best as minor interpellations are mainly applied for efficiency control of government and public service behavior. In the analysis, we address two major empirical challenges: First, we take into account the particular (short) time-series, (small) cross-sectional data structure incorporating dynamics as proposed by Bruno (2005). Second, in order to meet concerns regarding endogeneity, we apply an instrumental variable approach.

Baseline estimations

Table V.1 presents the first set of results for the full data sample including all three oversight instruments and observations from the old and the new German Laender based on the following equation:

$$\begin{aligned}&\ln(\textit{no. of interpellations}_{i,l})\\&= \beta_0 + \beta_1 \textit{fraction of ps}_{i,l} + \beta_2 \textit{mms}_{i,l} + \beta_3 X_{i,l} + \beta_4 D_i + \beta_5 D_t + \varepsilon_{i,l}\end{aligned}$$

where the dependent variable is the number of submitted interpellations or inquiries in natural logarithmic terms.[10] We include the fraction of public servants elected to parliament in state i in legislative period l as main explanatory variable. Additional explantory variables include, $mms_{i,l}$, a dummy variable being 1 if a mixed-member electoral system is applied, and $X_{i,l}$ capturing the additional determinants identified above. Laender-fixed effects are denoted by D_i, decade-fixed effects by D_t, and $\varepsilon_{i,l}$ is the error term.

Given that our dependent variable is logarithmized, we estimate specifications of a semilogarithmic functional form. Accordingly, the coefficient for a continuous variable shows the percentage change in the untransformed dependent variable per one-unit change in the explanatory factor. However, this interpretation of the estimated correlation coefficients does not hold for categorical (dummy) variables. As these coefficients are biased, we also report estimated mean coefficients (in square brackets) that are consistent, close to the unbiased results, and follow the interpretation of coefficients for continuous variables (Kennedy 1981).

10 If we do not transform the dependent variable, we have a count data setting. The negative skews of the three different dependent variables take values between 1.1 and 2.7 indicating only a slightly skewed shape. This does not require a model specification approach different from ordinary least squares. However, in our robustness checks with negative binomial models, we receive similar results.

Table V.1
Determinants of parliamentary control in the German Laender
Baseline estimations for all Laender
Dependent variables: ln(number of the different parliamentary control instruments)

	Major interpellations	Major interp.	Minor interp.	Minor interp.	Oral inquiries	Oral inquiries
Fraction of public servants	0.014***	0.000	0.070***	0.027***	0.024***	0.011
	(0.01)	(0.01)	(0.01)	(0.01)	(0.01)	(0.01)
Mixed-member electoral system	0.095	0.230	0.773**	0.367	1.435***	1.533***
	(0.23)	(0.24)	(0.33)	(0.28)	(0.41)	(0.44)
	[0.072]	[0.224]	[1.051]	[0.388]	[2.859]	[3.199]
Margin of victory	–0.005	–0.005	–0.016*	–0.014**	–0.009	–0.007
	(0.01)	(0.01)	(0.01)	(0.01)	(0.01)	(0.01)
New party	0.101	0.096	0.324**	0.227**	0.178	0.141
	(0.09)	(0.09)	(0.13)	(0.10)	(0.16)	(0.15)
	[0.102]	[0.096]	[0.371]	[0.248]	[0.180]	[0.138]
Number of parties	0.083	0.086	–0.396***	–0.223***	–0.170*	–0.076
	(0.06)	(0.06)	(0.08)	(0.07)	(0.10)	(0.11)
Seat share of the SPD	0.005	0.005	–0.028***	–0.012	–0.017	–0.024**
	(0.01)	(0.01)	(0.01)	(0.01)	(0.01)	(0.01)
Coalition government	0.410***	0.431***	0.252	0.242	0.488**	0.406
by major parties	(0.13)	(0.14)	(0.20)	(0.16)	(0.24)	(0.25)
	[0.494]	[0.524]	[0.262]	[0.257]	[0.584]	[0.453]
Constitutional parliament	0.317	0.238	–0.103	–0.480	0.984**	0.748
	(0.22)	(0.25)	(0.32)	(0.29)	(0.42)	(0.48)
	[0.340]	[0.230]	[-0.144]	[-0.407]	[1.453]	[0.884]

– Table V.1 continued on next page –

– Table V.1 continued –

	Major interpellations	Major interp.	Minor interp.	Minor interp.	Oral inquiries	Oral inquiries
Oral inquiries exercisable	–0.090	0.088	–0.496	–1.228***		
	(0.26)	(0.27)	(0.38)	(0.32)		
	[-0.116]	[0.053]	[-0.433]	[-0.721]		
Legislative period shorter than 1.5 years	–2.519***	–2.670***	–2.382***	–2.482***	–2.019***	–2.113***
	(0.22)	(0.22)	(0.32)	(0.26)	(0.45)	(0.45)
	[-0.921]	[-0.932]	[-0.912]	[-0.919]	[-0.880]	[-0.891]
Legislative period between 1.5 and 3 years	–0.662***	–0.622***	–0.348	–0.563**	–0.596	–0.692*
	(0.20)	(0.19)	(0.29)	(0.23)	(0.41)	(0.40)
	[-0.494]	[-0.473]	[-0.324]	[-0.445]	[-0.493]	[-0.537]
Legislative period regular 5 years	0.213*	0.206	0.742***	0.164	0.679***	0.906***
	(0.12)	(0.15)	(0.18)	(0.17)	(0.21)	(0.26)
	[0.228]	[0.215]	[1.068]	[0.160]	[0.930]	[1.391]
Laender-fixed effects	Yes	Yes	Yes	Yes	Yes	Yes
Decade-fixed effects		Yes		Yes		Yes
Observations	152	152	153	153	133	133
Number of Laender	16	16	16	16	15	15
R^2	.601	.649	.687	.823	.418	.491
Prob. > *F*	0.000	0.000	0.000	0.000	0.000	0.000

Notes: Partial correlations from OLS regressions. Standard errors in parentheses. Significance levels: * $.05 < p < .1$,** $.01 < p < .05$, *** $p < .01$.
For the instrument of oral inquiry, we have the information for 15 Laender. The Hamburg parliament documentation service does not separately document the use of oral inquiries.
In the estimation for the ln(number of major interpellations), we use a ln(major interpellation + 1) transformation in order to make use of the one legislative period, in which no major interpellation was submitted.
The values in square brackets accommodate the fact that we use a semilogarithmic functional form with dummy variables. The coefficients of the percentage change for all dummy variables are computed using the post estimation Stata command "logdummy".
Sources: See Table C.1.

There are two further general aspects concerning the specifications: First, there might be time-invariant factors in some Laender that are not captured by our independent variables but that systematically affect the use of parliamentary control instruments. We take this unobserved Laender-specific variation into account by including Laender fixed effects in all baseline estimations. Examples for such factors might be a Laender parliament-specific political culture or simply the size of the legislature that influences the use of the different control instruments. Second, we control for unmeasured time-specific effects on the use of interpellations and inquiries that might be correlated with some of the independent variables. For instance, there might be strongly disputed (political) issues in some periods that give rise to interpellations across Laender. Accordingly, we include decade fixed effects in panels II, IV and VI.

For all parliamentary control instruments, we find that a higher fraction of public servants is statistically related to more parliamentary oversight ceteris paribus. With regard to the size of the partial correlations, a one percentage point increase in the fraction of public servants in parliament is associated, on average, with a 1.4% increase in the number of major interpellations submitted (panel I). For minor interpellations, the effect is 7% (panel III) and for oral inquiries, 2.4% respectively (panel V). These results are consistent with Hypothesis 1, which emphasizes the lower individual control costs of public servants elected to parliament (given the level of political competition). Moreover, they also fit the qualitative analysis of Schrode (1977), who concludes that parliamentarians with a public sector background are more active and more critical in controlling government behavior during plenary debates than other parliamentarians. However, the baseline estimations are sensitive to the additional inclusion of time-fixed effects. For major interpellations and oral inquiries, we find that most of the variation that is related to the fraction of public servants in parliament can also be statistically accounted for by time effects (as shown in panels II and VI). For minor interpellations, the size of the partial correlations is also smaller. However, it is still sizeable and statistically significant at the 1% level (panel IV).[11]

In supplementary estimations, we analyzed the sensitivity of the correlations for public servants to potentially specific dynamics in the New German Laender. We therefore interacted the fraction of public servants in parliament with a dummy variable for the new Laender. We find no statistically significantly different effect for our main explanatory variable.

The partial correlations for the fraction of public servants are estimated taking a large number of other variables into account that control for potentially confounding factors. This is important because we draw statistical conclusions based on aggregate data thus facing the risk of an ecological fallacy.

For the further explanatory factors, we find the following partial correlations. The variable capturing a mixed-member electoral system is positively correlated with the execution of parliamentary oversight. This points in the theoretically expected direc-

11 In our empirical setup, including decade fixed effects could be too hard a test in terms of a type II error. We can only draw on 133 to 153 observations and there is common variation across Laender in the fraction of public servants over time.

tion – the more parliamentarians to be held personally accountable, the more effort is invested in parliamentary oversight. However, the coefficients have to be interpreted with caution. They are identified based on changes in the electoral system in only three German Laender. For the margin of victory, we find the theoretically expected negative sign. The larger the margin of victory is, the less engagement in oversight takes place. Legislatures with at least one new party are found to use more frequently instruments of parliamentary oversight. At least one new party in parliament is associated with 24.8% more submitted minor interpellations in panel IV. However, the partial correlations for the margin of victory as well as for new party are only statistically significant in the case of minor interpellations. For the number of parties an ambiguous picture emerges as correlations are positive for major interpellations (not statistically significant) but negative for minor interpellations and oral inquiries. No clear picture emerges also for the seat share of the SPD. The existence of a coalition government by major parties is associated with a more frequent use of all parliamentary instruments. The effects are quantitatively and statistically strongest for major interpellations. For the variable capturing constitutional parliaments, no statistically significant partial correlations are identified once decade fixed effects are included. However, an interpretation is difficult. With regard to the separate introduction of oral inquiries, the partial correlations indicate that there is a substitution effect of oral inquiries for minor interpellations. Not surprisingly, the length of the legislative period is statistically significantly related to the use of parliamentary control instruments. If we standardize the dependent variable by the length of the legislative period, qualitatively and quantitatively very similar results are obtained. Together, the explanatory factors account for 64.9% of the variation in the dependent variable major interprellations, 82.3% in the variable minor interpellations and 49.1% in the variable oral inquiries when including Laender- and decade-fixed effects. The F-tests indicate that the independent variables are jointly statistically significant.[12]

Refined estimations

In Table V.2, we concentrate on the use of minor interpellations, the main instrument for efficiency control. We restrict our analysis to the old German Laender with longer time series and address two major challenges. First, dynamics are taken into account in our (short) time-series, (small) cross-sectional data set as proposed by Bruno (2005).

12 As a further robustness check, we run the baseline estimations computing robust standard errors taking into account heteroskedasticity and serial correlation. We found qualitatively similar results. However, the calculation of robust standard errors traditionally presupposes a large number of cross-sectional units. This condition is not given in the present analysis since we only have 16 Laender. (Note though that recent contributions (see e.g., Kezdi 2004) show that the general robust standard error estimator (introduced to the fixed-effects estimator by Arellano 1987) also behaves well in finite samples.) Moreover, in our full sample the minimum number of observations per Land used to compute the disturbance of the covariance matrix is two for Mecklenburg-Lower-Pomerania and Saxony, and three for the other new German Laender. This small numerical basis renders the computation of standard errors unreliable and quite fragile. Due to these two concerns, we follow the conservative approach recommended by Angrist and Pischke (2009, chapter eight) and take whatever standard errors are larger (robust or conventional) as our measure of precision.

Second, in order to meet concerns regarding endogeneity, we apply an instrumental variable approach.

Table V.2
Determinants of minor interpellations in the old German Laender
Refined estimations
Dependent variable: ln(number of minor interpellations)

	I	II	III	IV
Lagged ln	0.577***	0.439***		
(number of minor interp.)	(0.06)	(0.07)		
Fraction of public servants	0.026***	0.012	0.098***	0.055**
	(0.01)	(0.01)	(0.01)	(0.03)
Mixed-member electoral	0.685**	0.561*	0.533	0.311
system	(0.34)	(0.30)	(0.30)	(0.20)
	[0.873]	[0.678]	[0.630]	[0.337]
Margin of victory	–0.011	–0.009	–0.015	–0.016**
	(0.01)	(0.01)	(0.01)	(0.01)
New party	0.336***	0.253***	0.190	0.180
	(0.10)	(0.08)	(0.14)	(0.10)
	[0.393]	[0.283]	[0.197]	[0.192]
Number of parties	–0.348***	–0.216***	–0.329***	–0.247***
	(0.07)	(0.07)	(0.11)	(0.09)
Seat share of the SPD	–0.005	–0.001	–0.039***	–0.019*
	(0.01)	(0.01)	(0.01)	(0.01)
Coalition government	0.226	0.253	0.189	0.133
by major parties	(0.21)	(0.18)	(0.21)	(0.16)
	[0.227]	[0.267]	[0.182]	[0.128]
Constitutional parliament			–0.019	0.277
			(0.35)	(0.22)
			[-0.079]	[0.288]
Oral inquiries exercisable	–0.224	–0.836**	–0.813*	–1.146***
	(0.35)	(0.33)	(0.34)	(0.25)
	[-0.248]	[-0.587]	[-0.581]	[-0.692]
Legislative period shorter	–2.724***	–2.744***	–2.395***	–2.456***
than 1.5 years	(0.25)	(0.24)	(0.47)	(0.34)
	[-0.937]	[-0.937]	[-0.918]	[-0.919]

– Table V.2 continued on next page –

– Table V.2 continued –

	I	II	III	IV
Legislative period between 1.5 and 3 years	–0.674***	–0.752***	–0.321	–0.550**
	(0.26)	(0.23)	(0.22)	(0.15)
	[-0.51]	[-0.541]	[-0.293]	[-0.430]
Legislative period regular 5 years	0.239	0.023	0.698***	0.090
	(0.16)	(0.20)	(0.22)	(0.17)
	[0.253]	[0.238]	[0.963]	[0.078]
Laender-fixed effects	Yes	Yes	Yes	Yes
Decade-fixed effects		Yes		Yes
Observations	122	122	134	134
Number of Laender	11	11	11	11

Notes: Specifications I and II: Dynamic bias-corrected panel estimator. Specifications III and IV: Instrumental variable estimator. Robust standard errors taking into account panel heteroscedasticity and serial correlation. Results are from the second stage of the two-stage least squares estimator. Instruments for the fraction of public servants are taken from the analysis in chapter IV. Standard errors in parentheses. Significance levels: * $.05 < p < .1$, ** $.01 < p < .05$, *** $p < .01$.
As the dynamic bias-corrected panel estimator includes a lagged dependent variable, we have only 123 observations compared to specifications III and IV. We lose one additional observation due to one gap in the time-series.
The values in square brackets accommodate the fact that we use a semilogarithmic functional form with dummy variables. The coefficients of the percentage change for all dummy variables are computed using the post estimation Stata command "logdummy".
Sources: See Table C.1.

Dynamic bias-corrected panel estimations

In panels I and II, we estimate dynamic panel models that explicitly include a lagged dependent variable. We apply the least squares dummy variables estimator for dynamic panel data proposed by Bruno (2005). This estimator corrects for the small number of cross-sectional units.[13] One possible driver behind a positive correlation of the residuals for consecutive legislative periods is the electoral advantage of incumbents. The average length of stay in German parliaments is about two and a half periods, see, e.g., Mielke

13 Nickell (1981) shows that the least squares dummy variables estimator (the common fixed effects estimator) is not consistent for finite T in dynamic panel data models. A number of consistent estimators, such as Arellano and Bond (1991) and Anderson and Hsiao (1982) have been proposed as alternatives to the least squares dummy variable estimator. However, the properties of the proposed estimators hold for large samples (large N) only. Bruno (2005) presents a bias-corrected least squares dummy variables estimator for dynamic (unbalanced) panel data models with a small number of cross-sectional units as it is the case in our empirical model. Here, the Arellano-Bond estimator is chosen to initialize the bias correction. We undertake 100 repetitions of the procedure to bootstrap the estimated standard errors. The results change neither qualitatively with a different number of repetitions nor when we choose the Anderson-Hsiao estimator to initialize the bias correction.

and Reutter 2004. Accordingly, the use of parliamentary oversight is partially influenced by the inertia of the personal composition of legislatures and the oversight culture that is carried over.[14]

As theoretically expected, there is inertia in the use of parliamentary oversight instruments. According to specification I, the elasticity with regard to the lagged dependent variable is 0.577. With regard to the political selection variable, the fraction of public servants in parliament is still positively related to the number of minor interpellations submitted. For a one percentage point increase, the estimated effect is between 1.2% and 2.6%. However, the effect is not statistically significant at conventional levels when we include decade fixed effects. The variable capturing a mixed-member electoral system is positively and statistically significantly correlated with the execution of parliamentary oversight in both specifications.

Instrumental variable estimations

In panels III and IV, we apply an instrumental variable approach to address concerns regarding endogeneity. This allows for the possibility that a third variable drives the fraction of public servants in parliament as well as oversight activities and thus generates a spurious correlation between the two variables. For example, a political scandal may increase voters' demand for parliamentary oversight, and simultaneously voters may also elect more public servants as legislators. To allow a consistent estimation, we instrument the fraction of public servants with the respective institutional determinants that are not themselves explanatory variables for parliamentary oversight. These instruments are taken form chapter IV. Panels III and IV report the results of the second stage of the two-stage least-squares estimation. We show one estimation without decade-fixed effects (panel III) and one with decade-effects (panel IV).[15] For IV-estimates, we calculate robust standard errors taking into account panel heteroskedasticity and serial correlation.[16] The fraction of public servants is again statistically significantly related to a more frequent use of minor interpellations in both panels. For the variable capturing the mixed-member electoral system, a positive partial correlation is found which is statistically significant in Panel III.

Altogether, we find throughout the specifications positive effects of the fraction on public servants as well as the mixed member electoral system on the use of minor in-

14 Since the variable covering constitutional parliaments always coincides with the first observation in a Laender-time series, it is dropped in the first and second specification.

15 The result of the first-stage estimation for the fraction of public servants (standard errors in parentheses) for panel IV including decade effects is as follows: -0.076 x strict incompatibility (0.035) -0.061 x soft incompatibility (0.037) + 0.069 x strict incompatibility x fulltime parliament (0.027) + 0.036 x pension benefit (0.021) + 0.084 x abeyance compensation (0.024) + 0.0694 x automatic promotion (0.036) -0.055 x other privileges (0.023). Compared to the analysis in chapter IV, the restrictive effect of the incompatibility regimes on the representation of public servants in parliament is less precisely estimated as we lose institutional variation in legislative periods for which we do not have data on the use of the parliamentary oversight instruments.

16 Excluding the new German Laender alleviates the problem of having too few observations in one panel in order to reasonably compute the disturbance of the covariance matrix.

terpellations. Both empirical findings are consistent with our two main theoretical hypotheses.

Based on our theoretical framework, one could further think of an interaction between the proposed selection and accountability mechanisms. In particular, public servants in parliament might face a stronger incentive to take advantage of their specific skills and information for parliamentary oversight if they are held personally accountable. This might be the case if they are directly elected in the majoritarian tier of the mixed-member electoral system. We tested this extension of the theoretical framework by adding an interaction term between the fraction of public servants and the presence of a mixed member electoral system. While a positive coefficient for the interaction term is estimated, the corresponding standard error is too large to derive strong conclusions.

5 Concluding remarks

In this chapter, we propose a framework to integrate the identity of legislators in a political economics analysis of parliamentary oversight. Legislators decide about the effort they invest in oversight activities depending on their individual control costs and the level of electoral competition. More parliamentary oversight is expected if the political process selects legislators with low control costs given the competition in the political market. Identity is thus understood as heterogeneity in control costs, which is driven by processes of political selection. This approach suggests that there is an interaction of institutions that shape legislators' accountability to oversee the executive branch and institutions that affect the selection of citizens into parliaments.

Our focus is on the political selection of public servants into parliament. In many countries, there is a debate about dual employment of federal and state legislators (see, e.g., Kerns and Martel 2008 for the U.S.). In particular, there are two countervailing arguments. On the one hand, public servants in parliament dispose of a high degree of expertise in public service issues and thus have lower individual costs of engaging in monitoring. Facing reelection incentives and individual accountability, public servants in parliament can serve as a check attenuating the information asymmetry between the executive and legislative branches of government. On the other hand, their double role as agents in the public service and as principals that supervise the public service in parliament generates a conflict of interest compromising their incentives for parliamentary oversight despite any cost advantage.

Our empirical findings for the German Laender parliaments support the hypothesis of a monitoring advantage of public servants. We find that overall a larger fraction of public servants in parliament is statistically associated with a higher number of submitted minor interpellations (our theoretically preferred indicator for parliamentary oversight). This holds when taking into account dynamics in the data as well as instrumenting the fraction of public servants in parliament with its institutional determinants. Moreover, we find a generally positive level effect of the mixed-member electoral system on the number of submitted parliamentary inquiries.

Based on our results, we think that it is worthwhile to study explicitly the use of oversight instruments in order to gain insights into the actual process of parliamentary control. In a next step, the current line of argument should be extended and outcomes of the political process should be analyzed. Altogether, the insights should provide a better understanding of when policy outcomes are more the result of political selection or the result of holding politicians accountable, and of when both mechanisms systematically interact.

Chapter VI: Consequences for Employment in the Ministerial Bureaucracy*

1 Introduction

The ministerial bureaucracy is mandated to draft law and it is responsible for the implementation of law and thus coordinates the public service. This top echelon of the public bureaucracy absorbs considerable public funds and public personnel and has grown enormously since World War II.

We analyze whether political economics factors impact employment at the top level of bureaucracy. We focus on the growth in senior official employment in the ministerial bureaucracy. Senior government officials are of particular interest since they are entrusted with the operational governance of the public service. Furthermore, they directly interact with the government and the legislature; either through close personal linkages or even personal unions.[1]

The functional approach to explaining the growth of the public sector focuses on demand-side explanations, such as changes in taste, income or the composition of the constituents. Complementary to this perspective, we investigate three political economics determinants and apply them to employment growth of ministerial bureaucrats. First, we ask whether the traditional partisan bias in policy choice matters for senior official employment. Second, we analyze how the changes in the composition of government that are indicative of party-political penetration in the top echelons of bureaucracy impact senior official employment. As a third determinant, we incorporate political selection. We focus on the role of public servants elected to parliament. Public servants in parliament compromise the separation of powers and thus face a conflict of interest. This is due to their double role as agents in public service and as principals who supervise the public service in parliament. Their professional interests might systematically bias legislative outcomes in favor of expansionary public budgets and inflated public-sector employment, including the ministerial bureaucracy.

We take advantage of a unique time-series, cross-sectional data set on the growth of senior public servant employment in the ministerial bureaucracies of the German Laender covering the time period 1957 to 2004. This data set is provided by Manow and Wettengel (2006). We additionally gather information on the ideological composition of the government, the change in the composition of the coalition government, and the selection of public servants into parliament.

We find no evidence for the traditional partisan hypothesis as senior official employment growth in the ministerial bureaucracies is not higher when a center-left govern-

* This chapter is a slightly modified version of the WWZ Discussion Paper No. 01/12 with the title "Determinants of Employment in the Ministerial Bureaucracy". I am grateful to Philip Manow for providing the data on senior official employment in the German ministerial bureaucracy.

1 For example, personal unions exist where there is no incompatibility rule to restrict public servants from simultaneously holding a legislative mandate.

ment is in place. We find some evidence for the impact of changes in the composition of governments on growth in senior official employment. This is consistent with political patronage considerations. Consistent with a special interest hypothesis, we find a positive correlation between increases in the representation of public servants in parliament and growth in senior official employment. In an explorative extension of the empirical analysis, this finding is, however, not confirmed if we try to additionally explore the long-run relationship between the representation of public servants in politics and the growth of senior official employment.

The rest of the chapter is organized as follows. Section 2 presents the theoretical considerations and gives information on the German institutional framework. Section 3 contains the description of the data set and the empirical analysis. Section 4 offers concluding remarks.

2 Theoretical considerations

Public sector growth is induced by either an increase in employment or in pay, or a combination of both. We concentrate on the employment aspect and select the senior-level officials in the ministerial agencies who form a politically sensitive high-profile occupational group within the public service.[2] Similar to the federal level, the senior-level officials in the ministerial bureaucracies of the Laender are entrusted with drafting legislation and implementing the law. Moreover, they are responsible for administering and for supervising most of the public service.

Before developing the theoretical arguments, we provide some information on the German political system. Germany (and its subnational jurisdictions) is a parliamentary democracy. Its governments are most frequently formed by coalitions, headed either by the Christian Democratic Party (the center-right party) or the Social Democratic Party (the center-left party) and sustained by a parliamentary majority. The smaller party (i.e., the junior coalition partner) is typically either the Free Democratic Party (*FDP*) or the Green Party (*Die Grünen*).

The German Laender have legislative competencies in public education, cultural affairs, public security and public administration which include the organization of the ministerial bureaucracies in terms of budget and personnel. The Laender government budget proposals must be ratified by parliament on an annual basis.

With regard to the employment conditions in the ministerial bureaucracy, it is important to note that officials enjoy public service status which guarantees their right to life tenure, fixed remuneration and promotion schemes.

2 We analyze the senior officials in the ministerial bureaucracy of the German Laender who are covered by salary class B(1-10). This includes positions such as the (deputy assistant) undersecretary/head of ministerial division (B1-7) (*(leitender) Ministerialrat* or *Ministerialdirigent*), the district president (B8) (*Regierungsbezirkspräsident*), the assistant secretary of state/head of ministerial department (B9) (*Ministerialdirektor*), and the parliamentary state sectretary (B10) (*beamteter* or *parlamentarischer Staatssekretär*). The prime minister (*Ministerpräsident*) and the minister/secretary of state of each department (*Ressortminister*) of the German Laender are not included.

2.1 Political partisanship

The partisan approach emphasizes that party ideology affects policy choice. Left-wing governments are expected to pursue a policy reflecting the preferences of their partisan voters. It is argued that left-wing governments appeal more to the labor base and favor expansionary fiscal (and monetary) policy.[3] Accordingly, they assign more competencies to the state. This might result in a larger state-production of goods and services which requires more public sector employment in general and more employment in the ministerial bureaucracy in particular. Compared to center-right governments, a center-left government will be less restrictive regarding decisions on public-sector employment (the ministerial bureaucracy included).

Based on this theoretical argument, we derive the *partisan hypothesis*: Center-left governments increase senior official employment in the ministerial bureaucracy.

Previous empirical research on the German Laender shows mixed evidence with regard to the effects of ideology on closely related issues, such as overall government expenditure, public debt and public revenue. Berger and Holler (2007) and Jochimsen and Nuscheler (2011) come to the conclusion that ideology does not systematically matter. In contrast, Schneider (2007) shows that center-left governments increase budget deficits. Focusing on single expenditure categories, Galli and Rossi (2002) find no evidence that government ideology affects the allocation of public expenditure. Oberndorfer and Steiner (2007) report evidence for a positive relationship between center-right governments and spending on higher education. Similar results are found by Potrafke (2010). Right-wing governments spend more on higher education and cultural affairs, whereas left-wing governments increase spending on the school system. One reason for the mixed evidence might be the ideological convergence of the Social Democratic Party (SPD) and the Christian Democratic Party (CDU) over time.

2.2 Political patronage

The allocation of senior-level positions in the ministerial bureaucracy to public servants who are partisan to the government's ideology is often argued to follow political cycles. On the one hand, this strategy serves the function of reducing asymmetric information and aligns the interests of the government and the ministerial bureaucracy. Public goods and services can thus be provided more efficiently as there are fewer obstacles in the multiple delegation chain (Strøm 2000). On the other hand, political allocation of senior-level positions to applicants with partisan interests conflicts with the principles of preserving a politically independent public bureaucracy that is recruited and promoted on the basis of merit. A politicized public service undermines the separation of powers and makes the abuse of sovereign power more likely (see for example von Arnim 1980).

We want to test if political cycles in the assignment of senior official positions take place after elections. We apply the argument to the following hypotheses:

3 See Blais and Nadeau (1992) and De Haan and Sturm (1994) for empirical evidence for a (center-left) partisan bias in fiscal policy, and Alesina et al. (1997) for monetary expansionary policy under center-left governments.

Political patronage hypothesis I: If there is a complete change in the composition of (coalition) government, an increase in senior official employment in the ministerial bureaucracy takes place.

Political patronage hypothesis II: If there is a minor change in the composition of (coalition) government, an increase in the senior official employment in the ministerial bureaucracy takes place.

The *political patronage hypothesis I* applies to situations in which the government and its sustaining parties change completely. The *political patronage hypothesis II* refers to situations in which the larger party sustaining government remains the same and only the smaller party in a coalition government changes. The *patronage hypothesis I* is supposed to have a larger effect on the growth in employment in the ministerial bureaucracy. There is also the reasoning that governments which anticipate losing upcoming elections strategically increase employment in the ministerial bureaucracy in order to either reward loyal partisan friends and followers with positions in the public service by means of patronage or generate partisan obstacles in the ministerial bureaucracy for the newly elected government. The latter argument is similar to the reasoning of strategic debt accumulation put forward by Tabellini and Alesina (1990). If such strategic increases in employment take place before elections, it is then more difficult to find evidence consistent with the political patronage hypotheses.

Manow and Wettengel (2006) investigate whether there are increases in senior official employment in the ministerial bureaucracy of the German Laender directly before or after elections that come with changes in the composition of (coalition) government. They find some evidence for political patronage when analyzing decade-specific developments of senior official employment.[4] Iyer and Mani (2012) analyze data on bureaucrat assignments from the Indian Administrative Service. They provide empirical evidence for the political cycle influence on bureaucrat careers in India.

2.3 Political selection of public servants

Recent research in political economics emphasizes that differences in the composition of the pool of politicians with regard to quality characteristics matter for political outcomes. We focus on one important quality dimension; i.e., professional background. This heterogeneity dimension fundamentally determines the personal socio-economic conditions that influence an individual's decision to run for office. More importantly, it shapes private economic interests and thus behavior once elected.

We concentrate on public servants in parliament. This single largest professional group in parliament poses a major challenge when considering the effects of political selection on public sector governance and public sector employment.

As proponents and representatives of the public service, public servants in parliament may favor policy choices that grant more competencies to the state and provide more

4 For a discussion of the politicization of the German ministerial bureaucracy from a public administration science point of view, see Mayntz and Derlien (1989).

services through public authorities simply due to their policy preferences. This results in a larger public sector including an expansion in public sector employment.

When analyzing public servants in parliament from a public choice perspective, an additional argument is put forward; namely the conflicts of interest. Conflicts of interest occur due to the personal unions and affiliations that are formed between the legislature and the public service. For example, persons holding both a legislative mandate and an executive position may face decisions as legislators that affect their role in the executive branch (for instance, voting on the budget of the proper department).[5] Public servants in parliament facing this conflict of interest may subject public sector employment decisions to less scrutiny or promote selective public service interests in the political decision-making process. As a result an expansion in public sector employment in general and in employment in the ministerial bureaucracy in particular might take place. For the ministerial bureaucracy, the conflicts of interest are immanent. In the case of personal unions, public servants elected to parliament are ministerial bureaucrats. Even without personal unions, conflicts of interest hold and are due to the frequent interaction between the legislature and the ministerial bureaucracy with regard to drafting and revising the law, and parliamentary control issues.

3 Empirical analysis

3.1 Data

In order to test the hypotheses empirically, we use a newly composed data set. We employ the data provided by Manow and Wettengel (2006) as the basis for the dependent variable. Manow and Wettengel (2006) carefully collect data on the high-ranking official employment in the ministerial bureaucracies of ten German Laender covering the time period 1957 to 2004.[6] In their analysis the (absolute) changes in senior official employment on an annual basis are examined. We adjust the data to identify effects on the basis of legislative periods. As we are interested in relative changes, we compute the growth rate of senior official employment in the ministerial bureaucracy; i.e., the percentage change in senior official employment for 116 legislative periods. We additionally adjust the percentage change of senior official employment for the length of the legislative periods. To explain the variation in the percentage change in senior official employment, we compile data relating to the political partisanship, changes in the composition of governments, and the representation of public servants in parliament as of the beginning of each legislative period. All determinants are assumed to impact growth in senior official employment until the end of the respective legislative period.[7]

5 If public servants elected to parliament are covered by incompatibility provisions that come with guaranteed reemployment, the conflict of interest is intertemporal.

6 Manow and Wettengel (2006) include Baden-Württemberg, Bavaria, Berlin, Bremen, Hesse, Lower Saxony, North Rhine-Westphalia, Rhineland-Palatinate, Schleswig-Holstein, and Saar. For the city state Hamburg no comparable data is available, and for the new German Laender no data has been collected.

7 One intuition for this assumption about the time structure is that politicians cannot implement their preferred policy immediately after election and rather have to implement it step by step over the whole legislative period.

Figure VI.1
Growth rate of senior official employment in the ministerial bureaucracy of Schleswig-Holstein per legislative period

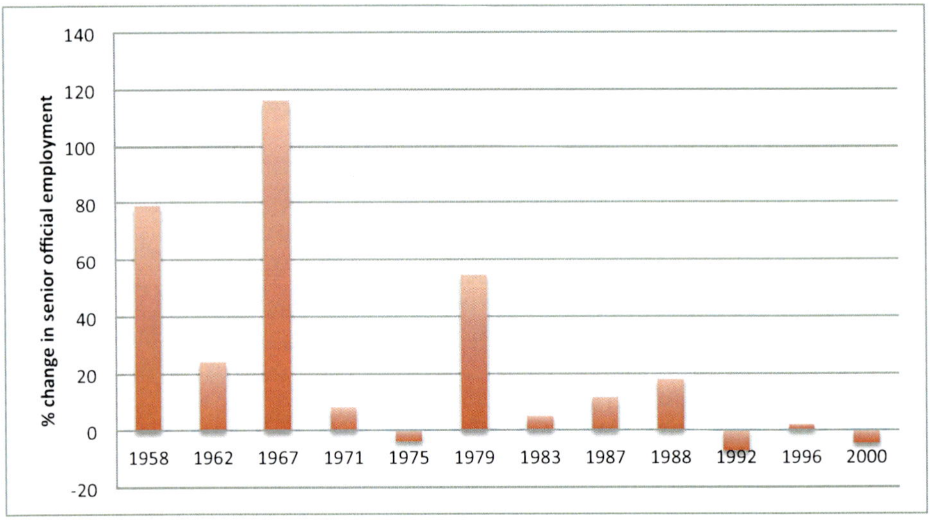

Note: The percentage change in senior official employment is adjusted for the length of the legislative period.
Sources: See Table D.1.

Figure VI.1 illustrates the growth rate in senior official employment in the ministerial bureaucracy of Schleswig-Holstein per legislative period. On average, the growth rate of senior official employment is 25.31% per legislative period - with a minimum of -7.23% in the 13th legislative period (1992 - 1996) and a maximum of 116.1% in the 6th legislative period (1967-1971).[8,9] The time series reveals strong differences between the single legislative periods. In particular, in the late 1960s an extreme increase took place. This is due to a general upgrade induced by a federal reform of the public service remuneration scheme (*Beamtenbesoldungsordung*). This reform was implemented in all Laender between 1966 and 1973.[10] In contrast, from 1983 onwards, we observe only small increases or even decreases in the growth of senior official employment.

---

8 Given the employment guarantee, a decrease in senior official employment is mainly due to retirement or resign.

9 With regards to the growth of aggregate senior official employment in the ministerial bureaucracy of Schleswig-Holstein, we observe 24 senior officials at the beginning of the 4th legislative period in 1958. The respective number at the end of the 15th legislative period in 2000 is 225. See Figure D.1 in the Appendix for a comparison. For all the ten German Laender included, in 2000, 4807 senior officials are counted in the ministerial bureaucracies. The respective number in 1960 is 524.

10 Between the late 1960s and late 1970s public labor law reforms brought about reduced work loads requiring an increase in public employment. For the same period, it is often argued that the government increased public sector employment to counteract increasing private sector unemployment.

Explanatory variables

The first variable takes political partisanship into account. Variables two and three try to identify the political patronage hypotheses. The last variable is aimed at political selection.

Government led by the Social Democratic Party (SPD): This variable capturing the political partisanship is coded 1 (0 otherwise) if the SPD is the only party or the stronger party sustaining the government in parliament. On average, 43% of the governments in the German Laender are led by the SPD.[11]

Major change in the composition of government: This variable takes value 1 (0 otherwise) if a complete change in the composition of the (coalition) government takes place. This is the case 12 times in our dataset.

Minor change in the composition of government: This variable takes value 1(0 otherwise) if the smaller party in a coalition government changes, but the stronger party sustaining government remains the same. This occurs 31 times in our dataset.

Percentage-point change in the fraction of public servants in parliament: This variable captures the change in the representation of parliamentarians with a previous or concurrent occupation in the public service. On average, the percentage-point change in the fraction of public servants in parliament is 1.19. In Bremen, the largest percentage-point changes are observed. In the election of 1967, the fraction of public servants decreases from 46.9% to 31.7% (a percentage-point decrease of 15.2). In the election of 1955, the fraction of parliamentarians with a public sector background increases from 34% to 55%.

The information on the political partisanship of government, the major and minor changes in the composition of (coalition) government is taken from Manow and Wettengel (2006) and complemented with information from the German electoral commission (*Bundeswahlleiter*). For more descriptive statistics see Table D.1 in the Appendix.

3.2 Estimation strategy and empirical results

We conduct our analysis in several steps. We present the partial correlation analysis from multiple regressions for the identified determinants of the percentage change in senior official employment. Basically, we encounter three challenges analyzing this data set: The small number of observations, the time-series, cross-sectional structure, and a reform period with extreme observations. The small number of observations sparks econometric concerns. However, information on the development of senior official employment in the ministerial bureaucracy for ten German Laender covering 116 legislative periods overall constitutes a unique data set and thus it invites an empirical investigation. As the number of observations cannot be enhanced easily, we, first, address dynamics applying dynamic panel estimators in Table VI.1. Based on this, we concentrate on the extreme observations within the reform period, introducing dummy

11 Situations in which the SPD is the senior partner in coalition governments composed of the two major parties are excluded. The partisan bias is expected to be weaker with two almost equally strong coalition partners.

variables for the reform period and respective interaction terms in Table VI.2.[12] In order to check the robustness of our results, we include demand-side factors in Table VI.3. Moreover, in a short explorative analysis, we look at the long-run relationship between political selection and growth in senior official employment in Table VI.4. For each step we briefly motivate the estimation strategy.

Dynamics

In panels I and II in Table VI.1, panel-corrected standard errors taking into account panel heteroscedasticity and correlation across panels are computed as proposed by Beck and Katz (1995). Dynamics are captured by incorporating serially correlated errors. As there might be time invariant socio-economic or institutional conditions specific to some Laender that are not taken into account by our explanatory variables but which systematically affect the change in senior official employment in the ministerial bureaucracy, we include Laender-fixed effects in panel I. Furthermore, there might be unmeasured time-specific effects on the growth in senior official employment that are correlated with some of the determinants identified above. As examples serve time-specific political pressures, such as high private sector unemployment or strong public trade unions inducing public labor law reforms. Since there is no comparable data on these variables over the whole time range of our study, these determinants cannot be included directly in the first place. Therefore, we include Laender as well as decade-fixed effects, taking into account both unobserved Laender and time-specific variation in panel II.

As we can see, no statistically significant relationships emerge that are consistent with our hypotheses on political partisanship and political patronage. Only for minor changes in the composition of coalition governments, do we find a positive - though not statistically significant - partial correlation which points in the theoretically expected direction. Consistent with our special interest hypothesis, we find a positive and - in panel I statistically significant - partial correlation between the percentage-point change in the fraction of public servants in parliament and the percentage change in senior official employment. As seen in the descriptive analysis for Schleswig-Holstein, there are strong differences in the growth rate of senior official employment between different periods. When we include decade-fixed effects in panel II, the variation in the dependent variable that is explained increases from 11% to 61%. However, when including time-fixed effects, none of the theoretically identified factors turns out to be statistically significant at conventional levels.

In panels III and IV, we estimate a dynamic panel model which explicitly includes a lagged dependent variable. We apply the least squares dummy variables estimator for dynamic panel data as proposed by Bruno (2005). This estimator corrects for the small number of cross-sectional units.[13] One possible driver behind negative correlation in the residuals for consecutive legislative periods is that an expansion in employment in

12 One might argue that a data set with extreme observations is more adequately analyzed applying a quantile regression approach. However, given the panel structure of the data set and the small number of observations, OLS seems a plausible compromise.

13 For a short discussion, see footnote 13, p. 95.

Table VI.1
Determinants of growth in senior official employment in the ministerial bureaucracy of the German Laender
Dependent variable: Percentage change in senior official employment

	I	II	III	IV
Lagged percentage change in senior official employment			–0.087	–0.452***
			(0.09)	(0.08)
Government led by the SPD	–7.340	–1.719	–4.787	3.868
	(8.37)	(5.65)	(11.28)	(8.38)
Major change in the composition of government	–13.760	1.173	–16.817	0.873
	(13.16)	(9.11)	(16.65)	(12.59)
Minor change in the composition of government	18.886	11.579	20.646	23.539**
	(12.08)	(8.49)	(13.18)	(9.66)
Percentage-point change in fraction of public servants in parliament	1.651**	0.554	1.888*	1.318
	(0.80)	(0.41)	(1.03)	(0.83)
Laender-fixed effects	Yes	Yes	Yes	Yes
Decade-fixed effects		Yes		Yes
Observations	114	114	106	106
Number of Laender	10	10	10	10

Notes: The dependent variable is adjusted for the length of the legislative period. Specifications I and II: Panel-corrected standard errors taking into account panel heteroscedasticity and correlation across panels. Dynamics are captured by incorporating serially correlated errors. Specifications III and IV: Dynamic bias-corrected panel estimator. Standard errors in parentheses. Significance levels: * $.05 < p < .1$, ** $.01 < p < .05$, *** $p < .01$.
The full sample contains 116 legislative periods (in 10 Laender). Including a lagged dependent variable leads to estimations III-IV based on 106 observations. Instead of 116 observations, we can only use 114 observations for specifications I-II. This is due to two early periods, for which we have no information on the percentage-point change in the fraction of public servants in parliament.
Sources: see Table D.1.

one period results in a more disciplined behavior regarding decisions on public employment in the following period. This might be due to budget constraints and the political feasibility of public sector growth. We estimate one specification without decade-fixed effects (panel III) and one with decade-fixed effects (panel IV).

The following empirical findings emerge from these refined estimations (panels III and IV). In panel III, the results are similar to the results found in panel I. We see a positive and statistically significant partial correlation between the percentage-point change in the fraction of public servants in parliament and the growth rate of senior official employment. The coefficient for the lagged dependent variable is not statistically significant. Only when we include decade-fixed effects in panel IV, do we find a statistically significant negative relation between a past increase and a current increase in senior official employment. The elasticity is -0.45 in panel IV. We, again, find no evidence for the partisan hypothesis.[14] Besides, we find a positive and statistically significant relationship between a minor change in the composition of coalition governments and the growth rate of senior official employment. This is consistent with the political patronage hypothesis II. With regard to the size of the coefficient: If there is a minor change in the composition of government, the growth rate of senior official employment is, on average, 23.5 percentage points higher. We find again no evidence for the political patronage hypothesis I which is assumed to have a larger effect on senior official employment growth. It is, however, difficult to come up with a consistent explanation for why we find no evidence for political patronage when major coalition government changes take place. For the percentage-point change in the fraction of public servants, the size of the coefficient diminishes by approximately one third and loses statistical significance when including time-fixed effects.

Reform period

Mainly due to a general upgrade the reform period (1966-1973) is characterized by an enormous expansion in senior official employment. In Table VI.2, we come up with two propositions on how to cope with the reform period. As basis, we take the specification III in Table VI.1 which puts strong restrictions on the data. One strategy is to include a dummy variable for the legislative periods affected. The other strategy is to additionally introduce interaction terms between the variable capturing the reform period and the explanatory variables. In doing this, we can distinguish between normal periods and special dynamics in the exceptionally expansive period.

Panel I in Table VI.2 repeats the specification III in Table VI.1 for a better comparability of the results. We find a sizeable and positive impact of the reform period on the growth rate of senior official employment in panel II.[15] We find a negative and - in contrast to the specification I - a statistically significant partial correlation for the lagged dependent variable. While once again a positive coefficient for the percentage-point change

14 We also extended our definition of the government being led by the SPD to situations in which the SPD is the leading partner in coalition governments composed of the two major parties. The results, however, did not change qualitatively.

15 19 legislative periods in our data set coincide with this reform period.

Table VI.2
Determinants of growth in senior official employment in the ministerial bureaucracy
Analysis for the reform period
Dependent variable: Percentage change in senior official employment

	I	II	III
Lagged percentage change in senior official employment	–0.087	–0.265***	–0.251***
	(0.09)	(0.08)	(0.08)
Government led by the SPD	–4.787	–5.951	–7.368
	(11.28)	(10.51)	(11.40)
Major change in the composition of government	–16.817	–14.662	–11.800
	(16.65)	(15.40)	(17.31)
Minor change in the composition of government	20.646	15.636	24.079**
	(13.18)	(12.33)	(12.20)
Percentage-point change in fraction of public servants in parliament	1.888*	1.389	2.097*
	(1.03)	(1.02)	(1.18)
Reform period dummy 1966-73		56.595***	75.338***
		(13.03)	(23.68)
Government led by the SPD x reform period			17.004
			(32.75)
Major change in the composition of of government x reform period			–26.948
			(72.06)
Minor change in the composition government x reform period			–32.482
			(23.79)
Percentage-point change in fraction of public servants in parliament x reform period			–3.277
			(2.96)
Laender-fixed effects	Yes	Yes	Yes
Observations	106	106	106
Number of Laender	10	10	10

Notes: The dependent variable is adjusted for the length of the legislative period. All specifications: Dynamic bias-corrected panel estimator. Standard errors in parentheses. Significance levels: * $.05 < p < .1$, ** $.01 < p < .05$, *** $p < .01$.

in the fraction of public servants in parliament is estimated, the corresponding standard error is too large to derive strong conclusions. A more sophisticated strategy to address the particular dynamics within this period is chosen in panel III. Here, we additionally include interaction terms for the explanatory variables.[16] We find a positive and statistically significant partial correlation between the percentage-point change in the fraction

16 Within this reform period, there is a center-left government in nine out of 19 legislative periods in place. Eight major government changes and one minor government change take place.

of public servants and the growth of senior official employment. The same holds for minor government changes. Within the reform period, we find partial correlations that have - except for major government changes - the opposite sign of the results found without introducing interaction terms. However, none of the estimated coefficients for the interaction terms reaches statistical significance at conventional levels.

Further robustness analyses

In Tables VI.3 and VI.4, we assess the robustness of our results with additional approaches. We again take the specification III in Table VI.1 as our basis. We extend our analysis in two directions. First, we control for growth in population, per capita income and unemployment. The inclusion of these factors aims at covering demand-side explanations for public sector growth. In particular, by including unemployment, we are able to test the argument that increased unemployment is counteracted by enhanced general public-sector employment which might be accompanied by an increase in senior official employment. Second, regarding the relationship between political selection and senior official employment growth, we execute an additional robustness check. In the preceding analysis, we concentrated on the impact that changes in the representation of public servants in parliament have on growth in senior official employment. This approach models a short-run relationship and indicates a positive association in our specifications. If we want to approach the long-run (equilibrium) relationship, one possibility is to add the fraction (the stock) of public servants in parliament to the estimation equation.

In Table VI.3, we include the percentage change in population (in panel II), in income per capita (in panel III), and the percentage-point change in the unemployment rate (in panel IV) as proxies for demand-side-based explanations. In all three cases, we lose observations due to the availability of information on the added control variable for early periods. We find a positive effect for the variable covering the percentage change in population. As theoretically expected, with higher per capita income, citizens demand more public goods and services. A 1-percentage-point increase in per capita income is associated, on average, with a 1.39 percentage point increase in the growth rate of senior official employment. We find no evidence for the impact of labor market developments as approximated by the percentage-point change in the unemployment rate.[17] For the determinants identified before, a qualitatively quite similar picture emerges compared to the preceding specifications. Throughout Table VI.3, we find a positive and statistically significant partial correlation for the percentage-point change in the fraction of public servants in parliament. Regarding the size of the coefficient, we find in specification III that a 1-percentage-point increase in the fraction of public servants in parliament is related to a 1.59 percentage point rise in the growth rate of senior official employment.

In Table VI.4, we further explore the relationship between the political selection of public servants and growth in senior official employment. Next to the percentage-point

17 We also checked whether changes in the demand-side factors are possible drivers of the strong increases of senior official employment within the reform period. Similar to the strategy applied in Table VI.2, we added an interaction term between the reform period and the respective demand-side factors. However, we found no evidence for systematic relationships.

Table VI.3
Determinants of growth in senior official employment in the ministerial bureaucracy
Robustness analysis for demand-side factors
Dependent variable: Percentage change in senior official employment

	I	II	III	IV
Lagged percentage change in	–0.087	–0.016	–0.120	–0.90
senior official employment	(0.09)	(0.09)	(0.09)	(0.08)
Government led by the SPD	–4.787	–9.178	7.728	0.912
	(11.28)	(11.11)	(7.64)	(12.17)
Major change in the composition of government	–16.817	–19.252	–3.972	–9.332
	(16.65)	(15.82)	(12.88)	(17.47)
Minor change in the composition of government	20.646	18.203	20.333***	26.104**
	(13.18)	(12.09)	(7.71)	(11.84)
Percentage-point change in fraction	1.888*	1.936**	1.589***	2.105**
of public servants in parliament	(1.03)	(0.94)	(0.61)	(0.83)
Percentage change in population		4.245*		
		(2.47)		
Percentage change in per capita income			1.393*	
			(0.73)	
Percentage-point change in the unemployment rate				–0.719
				(2.08)
Laender-fixed effects	Yes	Yes	Yes	Yes
Observations	106	100	85	98
Number of Laender	10	10	10	10

Notes: The dependent variable is adjusted for the length of the legislative period. All specifications: Dynamic bias-corrected panel estimator. The variables for population, per capita income and unemployment are adjusted for legislative periods. Standard errors in parentheses. Significance levels: * $.05 < p < .1$, ** $.01 < p < .05$, *** $p < .01$.
In specifications II-IV, we lose observations due to the availability of information on the added control variables in early legislative periods.

Table VI.4
Determinants of growth in senior official employment in the ministerial bureaucracy
Robustness analysis for political selection
Dependent variable: Percentage change in senior official employment

	I	II	III	IV	V
Lagged percentage change in			–0.186**	–0.436***	
senior official employment			(0.08)	(0.08)	
Government led by the SPD	3.179	2.294	7.304	7.383	4.247
	(7.76)	(5.90)	(10.11)	(8.39)	(11.65)
Major change in the composition	–7.557	1.495	–6.027	1.846	–5.842
of government	(11.03)	(8.86)	(14.54)	(12.33)	(15.56)
Minor change in the composition	14.503	10.788	18.138	21.407**	16.925
of government	(10.84)	(8.49)	(11.64)	(9.38)	(10.61)
Percentage-point change in fraction	2.590***	1.071***	3.135***	1.766**	1.985**
of public servants in parliament	(0.64)	(0.41)	(0.96)	(0.87)	(0.77)
Fraction of public servants	–2.186***	–1.030***	–3.222***	–1.200*	–2.888***
in parliament	(0.37)	(0.25)	(0.65)	(0.72)	(0.76)
Laender-fixed effects	Yes	Yes	Yes	Yes	Yes
Decade-fixed effects		Yes		Yes	Yes
Observations	114	114	106	106	114
Number of Laender	10	10	10	10	10

Notes: The dependent variable is adjusted for the length of the legislative period. Specifications I and II: Panel-corrected errors taking into account panel heteroscedasticity and correlation across panels. Dynamics are captured by incorporating serially correlated errors. Specifications III and IV: Dynamic bias-corrected panel estimator. Panel V: Instrumental variable estimation. Results are from the second stage of the two-stage least squares estimator. Instruments for the fraction of public servants in parliament are taken from chapter IV. Standard errors in parentheses. Significance levels: * $.05 < p < .1$, ** $.01 < p < .05$, *** $p < .01$.
The full sample contains 116 legislative periods (in 10 Laender). Including a lagged dependent variable leads to estimations III-IV based on 106 observations. Instead of 116 observations, we can only use 114 observations for specifications I-II. This is due to two early periods for which we have no information on the percentage-point change in the fraction of public servants in parliament.

change in the fraction of public servants in parliament, we include the fraction of public servants in parliament as a first step in exploring the long-run (equilibrium) relationship. We run the same specifications as in Table VI.1 and add the fraction of public servants in parliament. We again find a positive and statistically significant partial correlation for the percentage-point change in the fraction of public servants. However, at the same time, we see a negative and statistically significant partial correlation between the fraction of public servants in parliament and the growth rate of senior official employment. In the last panel, we apply an instrumental variable approach to further assess the long-run relationship between political selection and senior official employment growth in the ministerial bureaucracy. The instrumental variable approach allows for the possibility that a third variable maybe driving the representation of public servants in parliament as well as the growth in the employment in the ministerial bureaucracy, resulting in a spurious correlation between the two variables. For example, voters might demand more public servants as legislators and simultaneously demand more public goods and services inducing the government to increase employment in the public sector in general and in the ministerial bureaucracy in particular. To allow a consistent estimation, we instrument the fraction of public servants in parliament with its institutional determinants that are not themselves explanatory variables for senior official employment in the ministerial bureaucracy. These instruments are taken from the analysis conducted in chapter IV. Panel V reports the results of the second stage of the two-stage least squares estimation.[18] The result to notice is the following: If we only exploit the variation in the representation of public servants that is due to varying degrees of incompatibility regime strictness and compensating institutional privileges, we observe a negative correlation with the growth rate of senior official employment in the ministerial bureaucracy. The results of Table VI.4 might be interpreted in the following way: As more public servants are elected into parliament, more public service interests are asserted in the legislative process as approximated by increases in senior official employment growth. However, a strong representation of public servants in parliament (as measured by the fraction of public servants in parliament) is not associated with a permanently higher growth rate of senior official employment.

To sum up, we find, consistent with a special interest hypothesis, a positive and robust effect of the political selection of public servants on short-run senior official employment growth in the ministerial bureaucracy. When we additionally try to approach the long-run relationship between the representation of public servants in parliament and the growth in senior official employment, this positive relationship is not confirmed. We find no evidence for political partisanship and for political patronage after major changes in coalition governments. We find some evidence for the political patronage hypothesis for minor coalition government changes. The results are sensitive to the inclusion of

18 The result for the instruments for the fraction of public servants in parliament in the first stage estimation (standard errors in parentheses) is: -10.29 x strict incompatibility (4.38) -10.75 x soft incompatibility (4.40) + 12.14 x strict incompatibility x fulltime parliament (3.01) + 9.44 x pension benefit (1.80) + 8.45 x abeyance compensation (2.80) + 15.14 x automatic promotion (3.60) -13.35 x other privileges (2.03).

time-fixed effects and the variable capturing the reform period which indicates particular political dynamics.

4 Concluding remarks

The importance of high-ranking ministerial bureaucrats in the political process is undisputed in political science, administrative science, and in political economics since the contribution of Niskanen (1971). However, scientific work which addresses the growth of this politically sensitive and high-profile occupational group within the public service is rare. We take advantage of a unique data set on the growth of high-ranking official employment in the ministerial bureaucracy of the German Laender and examine it from a political economics perspective.

First, we analyze whether political partisanship has an impact on the growth in senior official employment. We find no such effect. This corresponds with previous mixed evidence on broader measures of public sector growth. Second, we investigate whether political patronage after major and minor changes in the composition of (coalition) governments takes place. We find evidence for such effects for minor changes in coalition government only. Moreover, we argue that the selection of public servants into politics is of particular interest for understanding how political selection affects public sector growth. Examining the effect that changes in the representation of public servants in parliament have on the growth of senior official employment provides evidence consistent with our special interest hypothesis, which assumes a positive relationship. A further explorative analysis, however, indicates that this result does not hold for the long-run relationship between the representation of public servants in parliament and growth in senior official employment.

The empirical results, however, have to be interpreted with caution as we encounter severe data restrictions in terms of the number of observations, the (short) time-series and (small) cross-sectional structure as well as a period of extreme observations.

Based on our results, we think that it is worthwhile to study explicitly the growth in senior official employment in the ministerial bureaucracy. In a next step, the current theoretical considerations could be analyzed for alternative outcome variables relevant to the high-ranking ministerial bureaucrats such as senior official pay and senior official job regulation. Related to the ideas by Alesina and Tabellini (2007, 2008), another highly interesting follow-up question is whether the growth in the ministerial bureaucracy is accompanied by a shift in the division of bureaucratic and political decision-making power from politicians to high-ranking bureaucrats.

Chapter VII: Conclusions

The research on political selection is an evolving field which raises questions so far neglected in political economy. In this final brief chapter, we summarize the essential results of the present book. Then, we discuss the implications for economic advice at the constitutional stage and conclude with implications for economic research.

1 Summary

In order to achieve good government, research in political economy has paid primary attention to the structuring of the principal-agent relationship between citizens and politicians and the role of competition in disciplining political agents. However, as political control and the credibility of policy commitments are limited, good government is also influenced by the identity and the quality of those selected for political office. We argue that a comparative institutional analysis of political selection is important and so far neglected in political economics. In our eyes, there are two crucial questions that arise: What are the institutions that systematically impact political selection; i.e., the composition of the pool of politicians with regard to quality? And, are there consequences for political selection and ultimately for political outcomes stemming from institutions that are primarily set up with the intention to hold politicians accountable? We therefore provide in chapter II an introduction into current research on the economics of political selection. We focus on the first question and discuss the selection effects of politicians' pay and of parties under alternative electoral rules. First empirical studies show that the ex-ante quality of politicians, as approximated by educational attainment, previous income or profession and political experience, increases in the salary paid to politicians (see Gagliarducci and Nannicini 2012, and Ferraz and Finan 2009). As regards electoral rules, we present the contributions by Galasso and Nannicini (2011a,b) and Mattozzi and Merlo (2011). They emphasize that the incentives faced by parties when selecting candidates depend on the nature of competition in alternative electoral systems. In the next step, we concentrate on professional background as one important quality and identity dimension of politicians. We select two prominent and well represented professional groups in politics, namely businessmen and lawyers. The few existing contributions by Gehlbach et al. (2010) and Rosenson (2006) show that institutions introduced to enhance transparency in politics, such as freedom of the media system and disclosure rules, are related to smaller numbers of businessmen in politics. Rosenson (2006) finds that institutional limits on client representation before courts are negatively related to the representation of lawyers in politics. Moreover, the empirical evidence suggests that particularly businessmen enter politics to promote their private economic interests when the institutional environment is weak. In addition, we point to further research questions. On the one hand, we propose to extend the comparative analysis of political selection to a broader set of institutions. On the other hand, we believe that the study of the interaction of institutional features is a promising avenue to take.

In the chapters III to VI, we further investigate the professional background of politicians and focus solely on public servants in politics.

As to the determinants of the strong representation of public servants in politics, we concentrate in chapter III on the major institution of incompatibility of a public service position with a legislative mandate. This institution has been primarily introduced to inhibit conflicts of interest and prevent the politicization of the public service and is traditionally considered an ex-ante disciplining device. For 71 national parliaments for the years 2000 to 2010, we compile a new data set on the incompatibility provisions in force and the representation of public servants in national legislatures. We find that the design of this institution matters much for the selection of public servants into politics. A strict incompatibility regime or an ineligibility regime (compared to soft incompatibility or compatibility regimes) is related to, on average, a seven percentage-points lower fraction of public servants in parliament. This is consistent with the theoretical argument that a stricter rule increases the opportunity costs incurred by public servants when pursuing a political office. Moreover, we prepare the grounds to explore the consequences that the selection of public servants into politics has on the political process and political outcomes. On the one hand, there is the concern that the conflicts of interest which rest on the personal unions and affiliations between the legislative and executive bodies as well as the perk of guaranteed reemployment lead to a strong and direct representation of public service interests in parliament. This is expected to compromise the efficient execution of public services. On the other hand, public servants in parliament form a pool of people with first-hand information about public service issues and a revealed interest in these matters. If this competence pool is partly excluded from the parliamentary process, we alternatively can expect a less efficient public sector. In the empirical analysis, the fraction of public servants is found to be positively related to the size of the government and the absence of corruption.

In chapter IV, we present a general political economics framework to analyze the cost-benefit calculus of a public servant running for political office in more detail. We extend the analysis conducted in the previous chapter with further institutional provisions applied only to public servants. For a newly compiled time-series, cross-sectional data set on the representation of public servants in German subnational parliaments, we once again find the restrictive effects (with larger effect's sizes) that incompatibility rules have on political selection. Moreover, privileges granted to public servants when pursuing a political career, in particular the compensation for holding one's office in abeyance and special pension benefits, are found to increase the representation of public servants in parliament.

In the next chapter, we turn our attention to consequences for legislative processes and study engagement in parliamentary oversight. We propose a framework to integrate the identity of politicians in terms of individual control costs. Public servants in parliament face a conflict of interest but also have lower control costs due to their experience and information advantage. The empirical findings for a time-series, cross-sectional data set on the German Laender parliaments support the hypothesis of a monitoring advantage of public servants. It is found that a larger fraction of public servants in parliament is associated with a larger number of submitted parliamentary interpellations. Overall, the possible conflicts of interest do not reduce engagement in parliamentary oversight.

Chapter VI analyzes the consequences for public sector employment. We test the hypothesis that the private economic interests of public servants elected to parliament systematically bias legislative outcomes in favor of expansionary public budgets and/or inflated public-sector employment. We concentrate on the employment aspect and select the high-ranking officials in the ministerial bureaucracy who form a politically sensitive high-profile occupational group within the public service. Based on a data set on senior official employment in the ministerial bureaucracies of the German Laender, we find, consistent with a special interest hypothesis, a positive correlation between increases in the representation of public servants in parliament and growth in senior official employment. This finding is, however, not confirmed if we try to additionally explore the long-run relationship between the representation of public servants in politics and the growth of senior official employment.

2 Implications for constitutional choice

Constitutional rules basically define the scope of action in a society. Constitutional political economy focuses on the question of how to design constitutional rules to meet citizens' preferences (see Buchanan and Tullock 1962, Brennan and Buchanan 1985, and Frey 1978). In order to achieve impartiality and "fair" constitutional arrangements (in the sense that they are of broad acceptance), decisions about the design of rules should be taken behind a (partial) veil of uncertainty. Instead of prescribing certain political outcomes for the subconstitutional political process, the constitutional political economy approach emphasizes the importance of the design of rules at the constitutional stage to properly shape the incentives of the involved agents at the subconstitutional stage.

This book is a contribution to inform the appropriate design of the (personal) separation of powers regarding public servants in politics as a part of constitutional choice. Referring to the selection of public servants into politics, we find statistically significant and economically relevant restrictive effects for the different regimes of incompatibility. Regarding consequences, we present mixed results. On the one hand, we see that the fraction of public servants in parliament is positively related to parliamentary oversight and to the absence of corruption (in the cross-country study). On the other hand, we find a positive correlation between public servants in parliament and the size of the public sector, measured once with government consumption (in the cross-country analysis) and once with senior official employment.

A regime of ineligibility as applied in the United States; e.g., mitigates conflicts of interest and thus reduces adverse effects on public sector efficiency due to either its sanctioning effect, its effect on political selection, or both. The U.S. Hatch Act defining the ineligibility provisions applied to public servants goes beyond other regimes as it aims

at imposing strict political neutrality of the public service. For most of the times, U.S. public servants were typically restricted from engaging in political fundraising, holding party office, taking part in voter registration and campaign activities in general.[1]
As reported by Snead (2001), stricter constraints on the political activity of public servants even favor the development of an aversion for politics, as indicated by public servants being less politically knowledgeable, less politically active and less satisfied with their public service activity. Moreover, an ineligibility regime aggravates the shortage of candidates often observed at the subnational or local level. Uncontested electoral races are likely to adversely affect political processes and outcomes.[2] One might also seriously consider shifting effects: Given that public servants face ineligibility rules increasing the opportunity costs of running for political office, the question of who enters politics instead arises. The restrictive effect of ineligibility rules on the selection of public servants into politics implies a further concern: If candidates from the public service with first-hand information about public service matters are partly excluded from politics, legislatures suffer from a lack of expertise when deciding about public service issues.

Taken together, jurisdictions declaring every public-sector position compatible with a political mandate run the danger of immanent conflicts of interest. Jurisdictions applying an ineligibility rule reduce agency problems either via ex-ante sanctioning or via selection, or via both channels. However, they simultaneously hinder a relevant and motivated competence pool of citizens from entering politics.[3] Accordingly, neither an ineligibility regime nor a compatibility regime appears to be desirable at the constitutional stage.
Concerning the design of political institutions in general, we submit that choices on the constitutional stage should be assessed not only with regard to how they solve conflicts of interest and contribute to individual accountability. Rather, constitutional choices should also be assessed with regard to how they affect the selection of people into politics.

In the subconstitutional political process, one should also be aware of partisan-strategic motives to introduce or reform political institutions which influence the selection into politics. Anecdotal evidence suggests that; e.g., U.S. Hatch Act provisions were proposed by the Republican Party in order to restrict the campaign efforts of the Democratic Party and to strategically tie the hands of the Roosevelt administration (see Bloch 2005). Another case in point is the current wave of introducing or tightening disclosure rules. These draft proposals are mainly supported by center-left parties which try to reduce the financial advantage of center-right parties, or at least put it to critical public

1 For an in-depth discussion, see Bowman and West (2009).

2 Miller (2010) even presents anecdotal evidence where the ambiguities about the exact provisions of the Hatch Act are abused by incumbents to deter potential competitors by threatening them with the loss of their public service position.

3 From a constitutional law perspective, an ineligibility regime gives the strict personal separation of powers preference over the constitutional right to equal access to political offices. This institutional arrangement is also regarded as critical by U.S. constitutional law scholars. See, for instance, the discussion in Bowman and West (2009) and Miller (2010).

scrutiny. A related consideration is put forward by Fiorina (1994) who argues that the U.S. Democrats pushed hard for the shift from part to fulltime state legislatures. The increased time requirements for the political mandate are less compatible with the professional backgrounds dominant among Republican candidates; i.e., especially lawyers and businessmen. Thus, the professionalization of legislatures supported by the Democrats aimed at making politics less attractive to many Republican high-quality candidates. Here again, our analysis provides relevant information to better evaluate the expected consequences of such (partisan-strategic) proposals.

3 Implications for economic research

Research on the economics of political selection is a new field in political economy. The contributions inspire with a new theoretical approach to study politics; i.e., the citizen-candidate model and the application of modern econometric techniques; e.g., the regression discontinuity design to recently accessible rich micro-data on politicians. The emerging literature sheds new light on established insights in political economy. In particular, political outcomes should be regarded as the result of discipline and selection. Moreover, institutions should be analyzed not only as to how they affect incentives and thus accountability in political office, but also as to how they alter the incentives for selection into politics in the first place.

Our contribution adds to this evolving field by highlighting one important (ex-ante) quality dimension of politicians; i.e., professional background. We select the prominent and single largest professional group in politics; i.e., public servants. In particular, we present empirical evidence supporting the hypothesis that the underlying institutional conditions systematically influence political selection. Furthermore, we offer evidence suggesting that the professional composition of legislatures matters for political processes and outcomes. We concentrate on the major institution of incompatibility (and related provisions) and introduce it to political economics research. Thereby, the complementary views of institutions in shaping both, incentives for political selection and for political discipline are emphasized. The results indicate that institutions primarily set up to hold politicians accountable influence political outcomes not only via the channel of discipline but also via the channel of selection. The insights, thus, broaden the basis for considerations about the constitutional design of political institutions in general and the personal separation of powers as regards public servants in parliaments in particular.

Not surprisingly, our own research results as well as the results of the contributions discussed in the review chapter provoke many questions and entail several avenues for further research. Apart from the (more specific) questions brought up in the discussion in chapter II, four issues should be accentuated.

First, a deeper knowledge of the functioning of often complex institutions in a comparative perspective seems extremely promising for a better understanding of political accountability and political selection. Second, more attention has to be devoted to the consequences of differences in the composition of the pool of politicians. In particular, the transmission channels from the selection of (ex-ante) high-quality politicians to improved policy choices and the interplay between selection and accountability mechanisms have to be further addressed. Moreover, the question of how to design political institutions in order to improve the selection process and attract "good" and especially publicly motivated candidates is completely open. A case in point is whether the remuneration rule for politicians is central in attracting high-quality candidates. As discussed in chapter II, recent contributions suggest that the (ex-ante) quality of politicians increases in the salary paid. Yet, before informing about the appropriate remuneration rule for politicians, a broader understanding of the relationship between monetary incentives and the selection into politics should be reached. For example, considerations such as the crowd-out effect of intrinsic motivation as proposed by Frey (1997) should be taken into account. A first set of institutions beneficial to political selection are proposed by Brennan and Hamlin (2000). They argue that institutions associated with the openness of government, such as open list proportional representation systems, freedom of the press and an institutionalized powerful position for oppositional parties are conducive to the quality of political selection processes. Finally, good government not only depends on the quality and identity of politicians, but also on the respective characteristics of decision-makers in other areas of government; i.e., in the bureaucracy and the judiciary.

References

Aberbach, Joel D. (1990). *Keeping a Watchful Eye. The Politics of Congressional Oversight.* Washington, D.C.: Brookings Institution.

Alesina, Alberto (1988). Credibility and Policy Convergence in a Two-Party System with Rational Voters. *American Economic Review* 78(4): 796-806.

Alesina, Alberto and Stephen Spear (1988). An Overlapping Generations Model of Electoral Competition. *Journal of Public Economics* 37(3): 359-379.

Alesina, Alberto and Guido Tabellini (2007). Bureaucrats or Politicians? Part I: A Single Policy Task. *American Economic Review* 97(1): 169-179.

Alesina, Alberto and Guido Tabellini (2008). Bureaucrats or Politicians? Part II: Multiple Policy Tasks. *Journal of Public Economics* 92(3-4): 426-447.

Alesina, Alberto, Nouriel Roubini and Gerald D. Cohen (1997). *Political Cycles and the Macroeconomy.* Cambridge, Mass.: MIT Press.

Alesina, Alberto, Arnaud Devleeschauwer, William Easterly, Sergio Kurlat and Romain Wacziarg (2003). Fractionalization. *Journal of Economic Growth* 8(2): 155-194.

Akerlof, George A. (1982). Labor Contracts as Partial Gift Exchange. *Quarterly Journal of Economics* 97(4): 543-569.

Anderson, Theodore W. and Cheng Hsiao (1982). Formulation and Estimation of Dynamic Models Using Panel Data. *Journal of Econometrics* 18(1): 47-82.

Andeweg, Rudy B. and Galen A. Irwin (1993). *Dutch Government and Politics. Comparative Government and Politics.* Basingstoke: Macmillan.

Angrist, Joshua D. and Jörn-Steffen Pischke (2009). *Mostly Harmless Econometrics. An Empiricist's Companion.* Princeton: Princeton University Press.

Arellano, Manuel (1987). Computing Robust Standard Errors for Within-Groups Estimators. *Oxford Bulletin of Economics and Statistics* 49(4): 431-434.

Arellano, Manuel and Stephen Bond (1991). Some Tests of Specification for Panel Data: Monte Carlo Evidence and an Application to Employment Equations. *Review of Economic Studies* 58(2): 227-297.

Banks, Jeffrey S. (1989). Agency Budgets, Cost Information, and Auditing. *American Political Science Review* 33(3): 670-699.

Banks, Jeffrey S. and Barry R. Weingast (1992). The Political Control of Bureaucracies Under Asymmetric Information. *American Political Science Review* 36(2): 509-524.

Barro, Robert (1973). The Control of Politicians: An Economic Model. *Public Choice* 14: 19-42.

Bawn, Kathleen (1995). Political Control Versus Expertise: Congressional Choices about Administrative Procedures. *American Political Science Review* 89(1): 62-73.

Bawn, Kathleen (1997). Choosing Strategies to Control the Government. Statutory Constraints, Oversight, and the Committee System. *Journal of Law, Economics, and Organization* 13(1): 101-126.

Beck, Nathaniel and Jonathan N. Katz (1995). What To Do (and Not To Do) with Time-Series Cross-Section Data. *American Political Science Review* 89(3): 634-647.

Becker, Johannes, Andreas Peichl and Johannes Rincke (2009). Politicians' Outside Earnings and Electoral Competition. *Public Choice* 140(3-4): 379-394.

Berger, Helge and Anika Holler (2007). What Determines Fiscal Policy? Evidence from German States. CESifo Working Paper No. 2062.

Bertrand, Marianne and Antoinette Schoar (2003). Managing with Style: The Effect of Managers on Firm Policies. *Quarterly Journal of Economics* 118(4): 1169-1207.

Besley, Timothy (2004). Paying Politicians. *Journal of the European Economic Association* 2(2-3): 193-215.

Besley, Timothy (2005). Political Selection. *Journal of Economic Perspectives* 19(3): 43-60.

Besley, Timothy (2006). *Principled Agents? The Political Economy of Good Government.* Oxford: Oxford University Press.

Besley, Timothy and Anna Case (1995). Does Electoral Accountability Affect Economic Policy Choices? Evidence from Gubernatorial Term Limits. *Quarterly Journal of Economics* 110(3): 769-799.

Besley, Timothy and Stephen Coate (1997). An Economic Model of Representative Democracy. *Quarterly Journal of Economics* 112(1): 85-114.

Besley, Timothy and Marta Reynal-Querol (2011). Do Democracies Select More Educated Leaders? *American Political Science Review* 105(3): 552-566.

Besley, Timothy, Jose G. Montalvo and Marta Reynal-Querol (2011). Do Educated Leaders Matter? *Economic Journal* 121(554): 205-227.

Best, Heinrich and Maurizio Cotta (2000). *Parliamentary Representatives in Europe, 1848-2000. Legislative Recruitment and Careers in Eleven European Countries.* Oxford: Oxford University Press.

Best, Heinrich, Christopher Hausmann and Karl Schmitt (2000). Challenges, Failures, and Final Success: The Winding Path of German Parliamentary Leadership Groups Towards a Structurally Integrated Elite 1848-1999. In: Heinrich Best and Maurizio Cotta (eds.). *Parliamentary Representatives in Europe 1848-2000. Legislative Recruitment and Careers in Eleven European Countries.* Oxford: Oxford University Press: 138-195.

Blais, André and Richard Nadeau (1992). The Electoral Budget Cycle. *Public Choice* 74: 389-403.

Blais, André, Donald E. Blake and Stephane Dion (1997). *Government, Parties, and Public Sector Employees.* Pittsburgh: University of Pittsburgh Press.

Bloch, Scott J. (2005). The Judgment of History: Faction, Political Machines, and the Hatch Act. *University of Pennsylvania Journal of Labor and Employment Law* 7(2): 225-277.

Bowman, James S. and Jonathan P. West (2009). To Re-Hatch Public Employees or Not? An Ethical Analysis of the Relaxation of Restrictions on Political Activities in the Civil Service. *Public Administration Review* 69(1): 52-63.

Braun, Werner, Monika Jantsch and Elisabeth Klante (2002). *Das Abgeordnetengesetz des Bundes - unter Einschluss des Europaabgeordnetengesetzes und der Abgeordnetengesetze der Länder.* Berlin and New York: Walter de Gruyter.

Brennan, Geoffrey and James M. Buchanan (1985). *The Reason of Rules: Constitutional Political Economy.* Indianapolis: Liberty Fund, Inc.

Brennan, Geoffrey and Alan Hamlin (2000). *Democratic Devices and Desires.* Cambridge: Cambridge University Press.

Bruno, Giovanni S. F. (2005). Approximating the Bias of the LSDV Estimator for Dynamic Panel Data Models. *Economics Letters* 87(3): 361-366.

Buchanan, James M. (1989). The Public Choice Perspective. In James M. Buchanan (ed.). *Essays on the Political Economy.* Honolulu: University of Hawaii Press: 13-24.

Buchanan, James M. and Gordon Tullock (1962). *The Calculus of Consent: Logical Foundations of Constitutional Democracy.* Ann Harbor: University of Michigan Press.

Bundesverfassungsgericht (1975). (Schluss-)Urteil v. 5.11.1975, BVerfGE 40, 296 [296-352].

Bunkanwanicha, Pramuan and Yupana Wiwattanakantang (2009). Big Business Owners in Politics. *Review of Financial Studies* 22(6): 2133-2168.

Bush, Winston C. and Arthur T. Denzau (1977). The Voting Behavior of Bureaucrats and the Public Sector Growth. In: Thomas Borcherding (ed.). *Budgets and Bureaucrats.* Durham, New York: Duke University Press.

Caillaud, Bernard, and Jean Tirole (2002). Parties as Political Intermediaries. *Quarterly Journal of Economics* 117(4): 1453-1489.

Calvert, Randy, Mathew McCubbins and Barry R. Weingast (1989). A Theory of Political Control and Agency Discretion. *American Journal of Political Science* 33(3): 588-611.

Caselli, Francesco and Massimo Morelli (2004). Bad Politicians. *Journal of Public Economics* 88(3-4): 759-782.

Chattopadhyay, Raghabendra and Esther Duflo (2004). Women as Policy Makers: Evidence from a Randomized Policy Experiment in India. *Econometrica* 72(5): 1409-1443.

Cooter, Robert D. (2002). Who Gets on Top in Democracy? Elections as Filters. *Supreme Court Economic Review* 10: 127-141.

Corey, Elisabeth C. and James C. Garand (2002). Are Government Employees More Likely To Vote? An Analysis of Turnout in the 1996 U.S. National Election. *Public Choice* 111(3-4): 259-283.

Cotta, Maurizio and Heinrich Best (2007). *Democratic Representation in Europe: Diversity, Change, and Convergence.* Oxford: Oxford University Press.

Couch, Jim F., Keith E. Atkinson and William F. Shughart II (1992). Ethics Laws and the Outside Earning of Politicians: The Case of Alabama's 'Legislator-Educators'. *Public Choice* 73(2): 134-145.

Dal Bó, Ernesto, Pedro Dal Bó and Rafael Di Tella (2006). Plata o Plombo?: Bribe and Punishment in a Theory of Political Influence. *American Political Science Review* 100(1): 41-53.

De Paola, Maria, Vincenzo Scoppa and Rosetta Lombardo (2010). Can Gender Quotas Break Down Negative Stereotypes? Evidence from Changes in Electoral Rules. *Journal of Public Economics* 94(5-6): 344-355.

Deutsch, Franziska and Suzanne S. Schüttemeyer (2003). Die Berufsstruktur des Deutschen Bundestages. *Zeitschrift für Parlamentsfragen* 34(1): 21-32.

Diermeier, Daniel, Michael Keane and Antonio Merlo (2005). A Political Economy Model of Congressional Careers. *American Economic Review* 95(1): 347-373.

Dietrich, Horst (1976). Beamte als Abgeordnete und das Diäten-Urteil des Bundesverfassungsgerichts. *Zeitschrift für Beamtenrecht* 76(4): 97-105.

Di Tella, Rafael and Raymond Fisman (2004). Are Politicians Really Paid like Bureaucrats. *Journal of Law and Economics* 47(2): 477-513.

Djankov, Simeon, Rafael La Porta, Florencio Lopez-de-Silanes and Andrei Shleifer (2010). Disclosure by Politicians. *American Economic Journal: Applied Economics* 2(2): 179-209.

Downs, Anthony (1957). *An Economic Theory of Democracy.* New York: Harper and Bros.

Eggers, Andrew C. and Jens Hainmueller (2009). MP's for Sale? Returns to Office in Postwar British Politics. *American Political Science Review* 103(4): 513-533.

Eschenburg, Theodor (1952). Der Beamte in Partei und Parlament. *Kleine Schriften für den Staatsbürger* 15. Frankfurt am Main: Institut zur Förderung öffentlicher Angelegenheiten.

Faccio, Mara (2006). Politically Connected Firms. *American Economic Review* 96(1): 369-386.

Faccio, Mara (2010). Differences Between Politically Connected and Non-Connected Firms: A Cross-Country Analysis. *Financial Management* 39(3): 905-928.

Faccio, Mara and David C. Parsley (2009). Sudden Deaths: Taking Stock of Geographic Ties. *Journal of Financial and Quantitative Analysis* 44(3): 683-718.

Faccio, Mara, John J. McConnell and Ronald W. Masulis (2006). Political Connections and Corporate Bailouts. *Journal of Finance* 61(6): 2597-2635.

Fearon, James D. (1999). Electoral Accountability and the Control of Politicians: Selecting Good Types versus Sanctioning Poor Performance. In: Adam Przeworski, Susan C. Stokes and Bernard Manin (eds.). *Democracy, Accountability, and Representation.* Cambridge: Cambridge University Press: 55-97.

Ferejohn, John (1977). On the Decline of Competition in Congressional Elections. *American Political Science Review* 71(1): 166-176.

Ferejohn, John (1986). Incumbent Performance and Electoral Control. *Public Choice* 50(1-3): 5-25.

Ferejohn, John and Keith Krehbiel (1987). The Budget Process and the Size of the Budget. *American Political Science Review* 31(2): 296-320.

Ferguson, Thomas and Hans-Joachim Voth (2008). Betting on Hitler: The Value of Political Connections in Nazi Germany. *Quarterly Journal of Economics* 123(1): 101-137.

Ferraz, Claudio and Frederico Finan (2009). Motivating Politicians: The Impacts of Monetary Incentives on Quality and Performance. NBER Working Paper No. 14906, Cambridge, MA: National Bureau of Economic Research.

Fiorina, Morris, P. (1994). Divided Government in the American States: A Byproduct of Legislative Professionalism? *American Political Science Review* 88(2): 304-316.

Fisman, Raymond (2001). Estimating the Value of Political Connections. *American Economic Review* 91(4): 1095-1102.

Frank, Sue A. and Gregory B. Lewis (2004). Government Employees: Working Hard or Hardly Working? *American Review of Public Administration* 34(1): 36-51.

Frey, Bruno S. (1978). *Modern Political Economy*. New York: Halsted Press, Wiley.

Frey, Bruno S. (1997). *Not Just for the Money: An Economic Theory of Personal Motivation.* Cheltenham: Edward Elgar Publishing.

Frey, Bruno S. and Werner W. Pommerehne (1982). How Powerful Are Public Bureaucrats as Voters. *Public Choice* 38(2): 253-262.

Funk, Patricia and Christina Gathmann (2012). How Do Electoral Rules Affect Fiscal Policy? Evidence from Cantonal Parliaments, 1890-2000. Forthcoming in *Journal of the European Economic Association.*

Gagliarducci, Stefano and Tommaso Nannicini (2012). Do Better Paid Politicians Perform Better? Disentangling Incentives from Selection. Forthcoming in *Journal of the European Economic Association.*

Gagliarducci, Stefano, Tommaso Nannicini and Paolo Naticchioni (2010). Moonlighting Politicians. *Journal of Public Economics* 94(9-10): 688-699.

Gagliarducci, Stefano, Tommaso Nannicini and Paolo Naticchioni (2011). Electoral Rules and Politicians' Behavior: A Micro Test. *American Economic Journal: Economic Policy* 3(3): 144-174.

Galasso, Vincenzo and Tommaso Nannicini (2011a). Competing on Good Politicians. *American Political Science Review* 105(1): 79-99.

Galasso, Vincenzo and Tommaso Nannicini (2011b). Political Selection under Alternative Electoral Rules. Mimeo. Milan: Bocconi University.

Galli, Emma and Stefania P.S. Rossi (2002). Political Budget Cycles: The Case of the Western German Länder. *Public Choice* 110(3-4): 283-303.

Garand, James C., Catherine T. Parkhurst and Rusanne Jourdan Seoud (1991). Bureaucrats, Policy Attitudes, and Political Behavior: Extension of the Bureau Voting Model of Government Growth. *Journal of Public Administration Research and Theory* 1(2): 177-212.

Gehlbach, Scott, Konstantin Sonin and Ekaterina Zhuravskaya (2010). Businessman Candidates. *American Journal of Political Science* 54(3): 718-736.

Goldman, Eitan, Jörg Rocholl and Jongil So (2009). Do Politically Connected Boards Affect Firm Value. *Review of Financial Studies* 22(6): 2331-2360.

Grant, J. Tobin and Nathan J. Kelly (2008). Legislative Productivity of the U.S. Congress, 1789-2004. *Political Analysis* 16(3): 303-323.

Grossman, Gene M. and Elhanan Helpman (2008). Separation of Powers and the Budget Process. *Journal of Public Economics* 92(3-4): 407-425.

Haan, Jakob de and Jan-Egbert Sturm (1994). Political and Institutional Determinants of Fiscal Policy in the European Community. *Public Choice* 80(1-2): 157-172.

Hain, Paul L. and James Pierson (1975). Lawyers and Politics Revisited. Structural Advantages of Lawyer-Politicians. *American Journal of Political Science* 19(1): 41-51.

Handschell, Christian (2002). *Abgeordnete in Bund und Ländern: Mitgliedschaft und Sozialstruktur 1946-1990.* Düsseldorf: Droste.

Herrera, Helios and Cesar Martinelli (2006). Group Formation and Voter Participation. *Theoretical Economics* 1: 461-487.

Hess, Adalbert (1976). Statistische Daten und Trends zur Verbeamtung der Parlamente. *Zeitschrift für Parlamentsfragen* 7(1): 34-42.

Hix, Simon (2004). Electoral Institutions and Legislative Behavior: Explaining Voting Defection in the European Parliament. *World Politics* 56(1): 194-223.

Holl, Stefan (1989). *Landtagsabgeordnete in Baden-Württemberg: Sozialprofil, Rekrutierung, Selbstbild.* Kehl am Rhein et al.: Engel.

Holthoff-Pförtner, Stephan (2000). *Landesparlamentarismus und Abgeordnetenentschädigung.* Baden-Baden: Nomos.

Holtmann, Everhard and Werner J. Patzelt (2004). *Kampf der Gewalten.* Wiesbaden: VS Verlag für Sozialwissenschaften.

Houston, David J. (2006). Walking the Walk of Public Service Motivation: Public Employees and Charitable Gifts of Time, Blood and Money. *Journal of Public Administration Research and Theory* 16(1): 67-86.

Imbens, Guido W. and Thomas Lemieux (2008). Regression Discontinuity Designs: A Guide to Practice. *Journal of Econometrics* 142(2): 615-635.

Inter-Parliamentary Union (2005). Chronicle of Parliamentary Elections. Vol. 39. Geneva.

Inter-Parliamentary Union (2007). Chronicle of Parliamentary Elections. Vol. 41. Geneva.

Iyer, Lakshmi and Anandi Mani (2012). Traveling Agents. Political Change and Bureaucratic Turnover in India. Forthcoming in *Review of Economics and Statistics.*

Jochimsen, Beate and Robert Nuscheler (2011). The Political Economy of the German Länder Deficits: Weak Governments Meet Strong Finance Ministers. *Applied Economics* 43(19): 2399-2415.

Jones, Benjamin F. and Benjamin A. Olken (2005). Do Leaders Matter? National Leadership and Growth since World War II. *Quarterly Journal of Economics* 120(3): 835-864.

Kalke, Jens and Peter Raschke (2004). Regierungsmehrheit und Opposition in den bundesdeutschen Landtagen - eine quantitative Auswertung von Plenarprotokollen. In: Everhard Holtmann and Werner J. Patzelt (eds.). *Kampf der Gewalten.* Wiesbaden: VS Verlag für Sozialwissenschaften: 85-106.

Kaufmann, Daniel, Aart Kraay and Massimo Mastruzzi (2008). Governance Matters VII: Aggregate and Individual Governance Indicators 1996-2007. World Bank Policy Research Working Paper No. 4654.

Kennedy, Peter E. (1981). Estimation with Correctly Interpreted Dummy Variables in Semilogarithmic Equations. *American Economic Review* 71(4): 801.

Kerns, Peggy and Luke Martel (2008). Dual Employment: Regulating Public Sector Jobs for Legislators. *Legisbrief* 16(10). Washington: National Conference of State Legislatures.

Kézdi, Gábor (2004). Robust Standard Error Estimation in Fixed-Effects Panel Models. *Hungarian Statistical Review* Special English Volume 9: 95-116.

Khwaja, Asim I. and Atif Mian (2005). Do Lenders Favor Politically Connected Firms? Rent Provision in an Emerging Financial Market. *Quarterly Journal of Economics* 120(4): 1371-1411.

Kintz, Melanie (2006). Daten zur Berufsstruktur des 16. Deutschen Bundestages. *Zeitschrift für Parlamentsfragen* 37(3): 461-470.

Kintz, Melanie (2010). Die Berufsstruktur der Abgeordneten des 17. Deutschen Bundestages. *Zeitschrift für Parlamentsfragen* 41(3): 491-503.

Klatt, Hartmut (1976). Die finanzielle Stellung der in die Parlamente der Bundesrepublik gewählten Angehörigen des öffentlichen Dienstes. *Zeitschrift für Parlamentsfragen* 7(1): 43-53.

Klatt, Hartmut (1980). Die Verbeamtung der Parlamente, Ursachen und Folgen des Übergewichts des öffentlichen Dienstes in Bundestag und Landtagen. *Aus Politik und Zeitgeschichte*. Beilage zur Wochenzeitschrift *Das Parlament* 44(80): 25-46.

Kotakorpi, Kaisa and Panu Poutvaara (2011). Pay for Politicians and Candidate Selection: An Empirical Analysis. *Journal of Public Economics* 95(7-8): 877-885.

Kriegbaum, D. (1967). Das Bayerische Rechtsstellungsgesetz und die Unvereinbarkeit von Amt und Mandat. *Zeitschrift für Beamtenrecht* 67(1): 234-250.

Kuniková, Jana and Susan Rose-Ackerman (2005). Electoral Rules and Constitutional Structure as Constraints on Corruption. *British Journal of Political Science* 35(4): 573-606.

Landtag Rheinland-Pfalz (1987). *Abgeordnete in Rheinland-Pfalz 1946-1987. Biographisches Handbuch.* Mainz.

La Porta, Rafael, Florencio Lopez de Silanes and Andrei Shleifer (2008). The Economic Consequences of Legal Origins. *Journal of Economic Literature* 46(2): 285-332.

Le Grand, Julian (2003). *Motivation, Agency and Public Policy. Of Knights and Knaves, Pawns and Queens.* Oxford: Oxford University Press.

Lengemann, Jochen (1987). *Das Hessen-Parlament 1946-1986. Biographisches Handbuch des beratenden Landesausschusses, der verfassungberatenden Landesversammlung und des Hessischen Landtags (1.-11. Wahlperiode).* Wiesbaden: Insel Verlag.

Levy, Gilat (2004). A Model of Political Parties. *Journal of Economic Theory* 115(2): 250-277.

Li, Hongbin, Lingsheng Meng and Junsen Zhang (2006). Why Do Entrepreneurs Enter Politics? Evidence from China. *Economic Inquiry* 44(3): 559-578.

Lizzeri, Alessandro and Nicola Persico (2001). The Provision of Public Goods under Alternative Electoral Incentives. *American Economic Review* 91(1): 225-239.

Lopez, Edward J. (2003). Term Limits: Causes and Consequences. *Public Choice* 114(1-2): 1-56.

Lübker, Malte and Suzanne S. Schüttemeyer (2004). Der Brandenburgische Landtag. In: Siegfried Mielke and Werner Reutter (eds.). *Länderparlamentarismus in Deutschland.* Wiesbaden: VS Verlag für Sozialwissenschaften: 137-168.

Luechinger, Simon, Stephen Meier and Alois Stutzer (2010). Why Does Unemployment Hurt the Employed. Evidence from the Life Satisfaction Gap between the Public and Private Sector. *Journal of Human Resources* 45(4): 998-1045.

Lundell, Krister (2004). Determinants of Candidate Selection: The Degree of Centralization in Comparative Perspective. *Party Politics* 10(1): 25-47.

Mallmann, Walter (1953). *Das passive Wahlrecht der Beamten.* Doktorarbeit, Universität Mainz.

Manow, Philip and Philipp Wettengel (2006). Ämterpatronage in der leitenden Ministerialbürokratie der Länder. Eine empirische Untersuchung der Stellenveränderungen vor und nach Landtagswahlen. *Die Verwaltung* 39(4): 553-570.

Mansbridge, Jane (2003). Rethinking Representation. *American Political Science Review* 97(4): 515-528.

Mansbridge, Jane (2009). A "Selection Model" of Political Representation. *Journal of Political Philosophy* 17(4): 369-398.

Massicotte, Louis (2003). To Create or To Copy? Electoral Systems in the German Laender. *German Politics* 12(1): 1-22.

Massicotte, Louis, André Blais and Antoine Yoshinaka (2004). *Establishing the Rules of the Game: Election Laws in Democracies.* Toronto: University of Toronto Press.

Mattozzi, Andrea and Antonio Merlo (2008). Political Careers or Career Politicians? *Journal of Public Economics* 92(3-4): 597-608.

Mattozzi, Andrea and Antonio Merlo (2011). Mediocracy. PIER Working Paper No. 11-002. Penn Institute for Economic Research: University of Pennsylvania.

Mayntz, Renate and Hans-Ulrich Derlien (1989). Party Patronage and Politicization of the West German Administrative Elite 1970-1987 – Toward Hybridization? *Governance* 2(4): 384-404.

McCormick, Robert E. and Robert Tollison (1978). Legislatures as Unions. *Journal of Political Economy* 86(1): 63-78.

McCubbins, Mathew, Roger Noll and Barry R. Weingast (1987). Administrative Procedures as Instruments of Political Control. *Journal of Law, Economics, and Organization* 3(2): 243-277.

Merlo, Antonio (2006). Whither Political Economy? Theories, Facts and Issues. In: Richard Blundell, Withney Newey and Torsten Persson (eds.). *Advances in Economics and Econometrics, Theory and Applications: Ninth World Congress of the Econometric Society.* Cambridge: Cambridge University Press: 381-421.

Merlo, Antonio, Vincenzo Galasso, Massimiliano Landi and Andrea Mattozzi (2010). The Labor Market of Italian Politicians. In: Tito Boeri, Antonio Merlo and Andrea Prat (eds.). *The Ruling Class: Management and Politics in Modern Italy.* Oxford: Oxford University Press: 9-107.

Messner, Matthias and Mattias K. Polborn (2004). Paying Politicians. *Journal of Public Economics* 88(12): 2423-2445.

Mielke, Siegfried and Werner Reutter (eds.) (2004). *Länderparlamentarismus in Deutschland.* Wiesbaden: VS Verlag für Sozialwissenschaften.

Milesi-Ferretti, Gian M., Roberto Perotti and Massimo Rostagno (2002). Electoral Systems and Public Spending. *Quarterly Journal of Economics* 117(2): 609-657.

Miller, Jason C. (2010). The Unwise and Unconstitutional Hatch Act: Why State and Local Government Employees Should Be Free to Run for Public Office. *Southern Illinois University Law Journal* 34: 313-357.

Miller, Mark C. (1995). *The High Priests of American Politics: The Role of Lawyers in American Political Institutions.* Knoxville: The University of Tennessee Press.

Moe, Terry M. (1989). The Politics of Bureaucratic Structure. In: John Chubb and Paul Peterson (eds.). *Can the Government Govern?* Washington: Brookings Institution: 267-329.

Moe, Terry M. (2006). Political Control and the Power of the Agent. *Journal of Law, Economics and Organization* 22(1): 1-29.

Nauber, Horst (1970). *Das Berliner Parlament.* Berlin: Colloquium.

Nickell, Stephen J. (1981). Biases in Dynamic Models with Fixed Effects. *Econometrica* 49(6): 1417-1426.

Niskanen, William A. Jr. (1971). *Bureaucracy and Representative Government.* Chicago: Aldine-Atherton.

Niskanen, William A. Jr. (1975). Bureaucrats and Politicians. *Journal of Law and Economics* 18(3): 617-643.

Norris, Pippa (1997). *Passages to Power. Legislative Recruitment in Advanced Democracies.* Cambridge: Cambridge University Press.

Norris, Pippa (2009). Democracy Cross-National Data. Available from http://www.pippanorris.com. Visited on November 10, 2010.

Norris, Pippa and Mark Franklin (1997). Social Representation. *European Journal of Political Research* 32(2): 185-210.

Norris, Pippa and Joni Lovenduski (1993). If Only More Candidates Came Forward: Supply-Side Explanations of Candidate Selection in Britain. *British Journal of Political Science* 23(3): 373-408.

Norris, Pippa and Joni Lovenduski (1995). *Political Recruitment: Gender, Race and Class in the British Parliament.* Cambridge: Cambridge University Press.

Oberndorfer, Ullrich and Viktor Steiner (2007). Generationen- oder Parteienkonflikt? Eine empirische Analyse der deutschen Hochschulausgaben. *Perspektiven der Wirtschaftspolitik* 8(2): 165-183.

Ogul, Morris S. and Bert A. Rockman (1990). Overseeing Oversight: New Departures and Old Problems. *Legislative Studies Quarterly* 15(1): 5-24.

Osborne, Martin and Al Slivinski (1996). A Model of Political Competition with Citizen Candidates. *Quarterly Journal of Economics* 111(1): 65-96.

Osborne, Martin and Rabee Tourky (2008). Party Formation in Single-Issue Politics. *Journal of the European Economic Association* 6(5): 974-1005.

Padro i Miguel, Gerard and James M. Snyder (2006). Legislative Effectiveness and Legislative Careers. *Legislative Studies Quarterly* 31(3): 347-381.

Pande, Rohini (2003). Can Mandated Political Representation Increase Policy Influence for Disadvantaged Minorities? Theory and Evidence from India. *American Economic Review* 93(4): 1132-1151.

Patzelt, Werner J. (1997). Sachsen. In Jürgen Hartmann (ed.). *Handbuch der deutschen Bundesländer.* Frankfurt/New York: Campus: 503-545.

Patzelt, Werner J. (1999). Recruitment and Retention in Western European Parliaments. *Legislative Studies Quarterly* 24(2): 239-279.

Patzelt, Werner (2005). *Parlamente und ihre Macht.* Kategorien und Fallbeispiele institutioneller Analyse. Baden-Baden: Nomos.

Patzelt, Werner (2006). Länderparlamentarismus. In: Herbert Schneider and Hans-Georg Wehling (eds.). *Landespolitik in Deutschland. Grundlagen-Strukturen-Arbeitsfelder.* Wiesbaden: VS Verlag für Sozialwissenschaften: 108-129.

Persson, Torsten and Guido Tabellini (2005). *The Economic Effects of Constitutions.* Cambridge: MIT Press.

Persson, Torsten, Roland Gerard and Guido Tabellini (1997). Separation of Powers and Political Accountability. *Quarterly Journal of Economics* 112(4): 1163-1202.

Persson, Torsten, Guido Tabellini and Francesco Trebbi (2003). Electoral Rules and Corruption. *Journal of the European Economic Association* 1(4): 958-989.

Pitkin, Hanna F. (1967). *The Concept of Representation.* Berkeley: University of California Press.

Podmore, David (1977). Lawyers and Politics. *British Journal of Law and Society* 4(2): 155-185.

Potrafke, Niklas (2010). Public Expenditures on Education and Cultural Affairs in the West German States: Does Government Ideology Influence the Budget Composition? *German Economic Review* 12(1): 124-145.

Raschke, Peter and Jens Kalke (1994). Quantitative Analyse parlamentarischer Tätigkeiten der Landtage. *Zeitschrift für Parlamentsfragen* 25(1): 32-45.

Reutter, Werner (2008). *Föderalismus, Parlamentarismus und Demokratie. Landesparlamente im Bundesstaat.* Opladen and Farmington Hills: Verlag Barbara Budrich.

Rosenson, Beth (2006). The Impact of Ethics Laws on Legislative Recruitment and the Occupational Composition of State Legislatures. *Political Research Quarterly* 59(4): 619-627.

Rosenthal, Alan (1981). Legislative Behavior and Legislative Oversight. *Legislative Studies Quarterly* 6(1): 115-131.

Russo, Federico and Matti Wiberg. (2010). Parliamentary Questioning in 17 European Parliaments: Some Steps Towards Comparison. *Journal of Legislative Studies* 16(2): 215-232.

Rütters, Peter (2003). Daten zur Sozialstruktur des saarländischen Landtages 1947-1999. *Zeitschrift für Parlamentsfragen* 34(1): 95-115.

Schäfer, Markus (2005). *Datenhandbuch zur Geschichte des Landtags Rheinland-Pfalz 1947-2003.* Mainz: Hase & Koehler.

Scheuch, Erwin K. and Ute Scheuch (1992). *Cliquen, Klüngel und Karrieren.* Reinbek: Rowohlt.

Schindler, Peter (1999). *Datenhandbuch zur Geschichte des Deutschen Bundestages 1949-1999.* Baden-Baden: Nomos.

Schlesinger, Joseph A. (1957). Lawyers and American Politics: A Clarified View. *Midwest Journal of Political Science.* 1(1): 26-39.

Schmidt, Walther, W. (1970). Die Unvereinbarkeit von Parlamentsmandat und Exekutivfunktionen in ausländischen Rechtsordnungen. *Zeitschrift für Parlamentsfragen* 2(2): 181-191.

Schneider, Christina J. (2007). Political Opportunism and Budget Deficits in the West-German Länder. *Politische Vierteljahresschrift* 48(2): 221-242.

Schrode, Klaus (1977). *Beamtenabgeordnete in Landtagen der Bundesrepublik Deutschland.* Heidelberg: Carl Winter Universitätsverlag.

Schwartz, Nancy L. (1988). *The Blue Guitar: Political Representation and Community.* Chicago: University of Chicago Press.

Serna, Angel (1995). *Selektionseffekte bei der Kandidatenauswahl. Bedeutung, Funktionsweise und Konsequenzen. Eine ökonomische Analyse der Märkte für Politiker.* Chur/Zürich: Ruegger.

Serra, Danila (2006). Empirical Determinants of Corruption: A Sensitivity Analysis. *Public Choice* 126(1-2): 225-256.

Shapiro, Carl and Joseph E. Stiglitz (1984). Equilibrium Unemployment as a Worker Discipline Device. *American Economic Review* 74(3): 433-444.

Shelton, Cameron A. (2007). The Size and Composition of Government Expenditure. *Journal of Public Economics* 91(11-12): 2230-2260.

Shiller, Wendy J. (1995). Senators as Political Entrepreneurs: Using Bill Sponsorship to Shape Legislative Agendas. *American Journal of Political Science* 39(1): 186-203.

Snead, John D. (2001). An Inquiry Into the Chilling Effects of Stringent Little Hatch Act Prohibitions. *Review of Public Personnel Administration* 21(4): 259-283.

Snyder, James M. and Michael M. Ting (2002). An Informational Rationale for Political Parties. *American Journal of Political Science* 46(1): 90-110.

Statistisches Bundesamt Deutschland (2005). *Deutschland in Zahlen.* Bonn.

Strøm, Kaare (2000). Delegation and Accountability in Parliamentary Democracies. *European Journal of Political Research* 37(3): 261-290.

Sturm, Gerd (1967). *Die Inkompatibilität: Eine Studie zum Problem der Unvereinbarkeiten im geltenden deutschen Staatsrecht.* München: C. H. Beck'sche Verlagsbuchhandlung.

Tabellini, Guido and Alberto Alesina (1990). Voting on the Budget Deficit. *American Economic Review* 80(1): 37-49.

Thüringer Landtag (2005). Der Thüringer Landtag und seine Abgeordneten 1990-2005. Studien zu 15 Jahren Landesparlamentarismus. *Schriften zur Geschichte des Parlamentarismus in Thüringen* 24. Erfurt: Hain Verlag.

Treisman, Daniel (2007). What Have We Learned About the Causes of Corruption from Ten Years of Cross-National Empirical Research? *Annual Review of Political Science* 10(6): 211-244.

Tsatsos, Dimitris Th. (1970). *Die parlamentarische Inkompatibilität von öffentlichen Bediensteten.* Bad Homburg, Berlin and Zürich: Gehlen.

Tullock, Gordon (1965). *The Politics of Bureaucracy.* Washington D. C.: Public Affairs Press.

van Aaken, Anne (2005). Genügt das deutsche Recht den Anforderungen der VN-Konvention gegen Korruption? Eine rechtsvergleichende Studie zur politischen Korruption unter besonderer Berücksichtigung der Rechtslage in Deutschland. *Zeitschrift für ausländisches öffentliches Recht und Völkerrecht* 65(2): 407-446.

van Aaken, Anne and Stefan Voigt (2011). Do Individual Disclosure Rules for Parliamentarians Improve Government Effectiveness? *Economics of Governance* 12(4): 301-324.

van der Hulst, Marc (2000). The Parliamentary Mandate. A Global Perspective. Geneva: Inter-Parliamentary Union.

von Arnim, Hans H. (1980). *Ämterpatronage durch politische Parteien.* Wiesbaden: Karl-Bräuer-Institut des Bundes der Steuerzahler.

von Arnim, Hans H. (1991). *Die Partei, der Abgeordnete und das Geld.* Mainz: Koehler.

von Arnim, Hans H. (2006). Parteien in der Kritik. *Zeitschrift für öffentliches Recht und Verwaltungswissenschaft* 60(6): 222-229.

Volkshandbücher of the German Laender parliaments Baden-Württemberg, Bavaria, Berlin, Hesse, Rhineland-Palatinate, Saar, Schleswig-Holstein, North Rhine-Westphalia, Saxony, Lower Saxony, Bremen, Hamburg, Brandenburg, Saxony-Anhalt and Mecklenburg-Lower-Pomerania. Rheinbreitbach: Neue Darmstädter Verlags-anstalt.

Weingast, Barry R. (1984). The Congressional-Bureaucratic System: A Principal-Agent Perspective (with Applications to the SEC). *Public Choice* 44(1): 147-191.

Weingast, Barry R. and Mark Moran (1983). Bureaucratic Discretion or Congressional Control? Regulatory Policymaking by the Federal Trade Commission. *Journal of Political Economy* 91(5): 765-800.

Weiss, Andrew (1980). Job Queues and Layoffs in Labor Markets with Flexible Wages. *Journal of Political Economy* 88(3): 526-538.

Wittman, Donald (1977). Candidates with Policy Preferences: A Dynamic Model. *Journal of Economic Theory* 14(1): 180-189.

Wittman, Donald (1983). Candidate Motivation: A Synthesis of Alternative Theories. *American Political Science Review* 77(1): 142-157.

Yamamoto, Hironori (2007). Tools for Parliamentary Oversight. A Comparative Study of 88 National Parliaments. Geneva: Inter-Parliamentary Union.

Appendix

Appendix A

Table A.1a
Occupational composition of the United Kingdom House of the Commons elected in 2005

	#	Fraction
Public sector		
Professors or lecturers	44	0.0715
Teachers	47	0.0764
Scientists	7	0.0114
Civil servants	28	0.0455
Military/police officers	14	0.0228
Total	140	0.2276
Professions related to political activities		
Professional politicians or professions related to political activities	87	0.1415
Other sectors		
Barristers, solicitors, lawyers	72	0.1171
Architects	7	0.0114
Engineers	5	0.0081
Medical professions	6	0.0098
Consultants	2	0.0033
Business, trade, and industry employees, including executives	118	0.1919
Media writers, publishers, broadcasters and producers	43	0.0699
Accountants	10	0.0163
Employees of Private Company	78	0.1268
Farmers	8	0.0130
Manual workers	38	0.0618
Total	387	0.6293
Others		
Housewives	1	0.0016
Total	615	1

Notes: The statistic covers 615 seats held by the three main parties (Labour, Conservatives and Liberal Democrats) out of a total of 646 seats.
Source: Inter-Parliamentary Union (2005).

Table A.1b
Occupational composition of the Algerian Parliament in 2007

	#	Fraction
Public sector		
Public servants and public administrators	131	0.3368
Educators	56	0.1440
Military and police officers	3	0.0077
Scientists and researchers	1	0.0026
Total	191	0.4910
Other sectors		
Legal professions	30	0.0771
Medical professions (doctors, dentists, nurses)	20	0.0514
Liberal professions (including artists, authors) and sport professionals	37	0.0951
Consultants (including real estate agents)	13	0.0334
Business, trade, and industry employees, including executives	12	0.0308
Bankers (including investment bankers) and accountants	7	0.0180
Media-related professions (journalists and publishers)	2	0.0051
Farmers and agricultural workers (including wine growers)	2	0.0051
Economists	1	0.0026
Total	124	0.3188
Others		
Retired	31	0.0797
Unemployed	2	0.0051
Total	33	0.0848
Unknown	41	0.1054
Total	389	1

Notes: The category "public servants and public administrators" includes social and development workers.
Source: Inter-Parliamentary Union (2007).

Table A.1c
Occupational composition of the 17th German Parliament (*Bundestag*) elected in 2009

	#	Fraction
1. Employed		
1.1 Public service (public servants and employees in the public service)		
Public administration	62	0.0997
Police	7	0.0113
Judiciary	13	0.0209
Military	3	0.0048
Municipal public servants	13	0.0209
Educational professions and researchers	86	0.1383
Medical professions	9	0.0145
Others	6	0.0096
Total	199	0.3199
1.2 Professions related to political activities		
Employees of parties	36	0.0579
Employees of trade unions	24	0.0386
Former employees of parliamentarians	14	0.0225
Others	16	0.0257
Total	90	0.1447
1.3 Private sector employees including employees of professional associations		
Employees in artisanry, manufacturing, industry, sales and services	54	0.0868
Agricultural workers	1	0.0016
Employees in financial sector	6	0.0096
Insurance employees	2	0.0032
Media employees	14	0.0225
Others	20	0.0322
Total	97	0.1559
2. Self-employed		
2.1 Liberal professions		
Legal professions	102	0.1640
Medical professions	4	0.0064
Media-related professions	21	0.0338
Liberal technical professions	4	0.0064
Other liberal professions	7	0.0113
Total	138	0.2219

– continued on next page –

Table A.1c – continued

2.2 Other self-employed		
Self-employed in artisanry, manufacturing, industry, sales and services	32	0.0514
Farmers	11	0.0177
Insurance broker	3	0.0048
Others	3	0.0048
Total	49	0.0788
3. Others		
Housewives	2	0.0032
Students or in apprenticeship	8	0.0129
Clerical professions	6	0.0096
Total	16	0.0257
4. Unknown	33	0.0531
Total	622	1

Source: German parliamentary online service.

Table A.2
Data sources and descriptive statistics for the fraction of public servants in national parliaments

Country	Year of election	Fraction of public servants in %	
		Adjusted	Unadjusted
Own coding based on national parliamentary statistics			
Albania	2001	24.42	22.14
Austria	2008	33.88	33.88
Germany	2009	33.78	31.99
Italy	2008	19.97	19.97
Own coding based on the national parliamentary online data bases containing detailed and systematic individual information			
Canada	2006	19.87	19.87
Finland	2008	46.49	43.00
Ireland	2007	31.55	31.55
Israel	2009	29.87	19.17
Netherlands	2010	32.39	30.67
Own coding based on the individual MP's webpage (without systematic information)			
United States of America	2008	33.10	32.65
Own coding based on Inter-Parliamentary Union statistics for national parliaments			
Algeria	2007	54.88	49.10
Andorra	2005	19.23	17.86
Argentina	2007	18.69	16.86
Armenia	2007	17.56	17.56
Australia	2004	18.00	18.00
Azerbaijan	2005	27.44	26.96
Belarus	2004	37.97	27.27
Belgium	2007	25.18	24.00
Bosnia and Herzegovina	2002	9.52	9.52
Bulgaria	2005	20.26	18.08
Burkina Faso	2002	45.05	45.05
Burundi	2005	48.31	48.31
Central African Republic	2005	44.66	43.81
Chile	2009	20.83	20.83
Congo, Rep.	2007	34.45	22.63
Cyprus	2006	21.82	21.43
Denmark	2007	53.99	49.16
Djibouti	2008	73.85	73.85
Dominica	2005	28.58	25.81
Egypt, Arab Rep.	2007	26.16	24.61
Estonia	2007	41.23	39.60
France	2007	34.34	29.64

– continued on next page –

Table A.2 – continued

Gambia	2002	48.08	47.17
Greece	2007	18.67	18.67
Haiti	2006	31.03	27.55
Hungary	2006	26.63	25.39
Indonesia	2004	9.58	9.27
Kuwait	2006	56.52	40.00
Latvia	2006	45.00	45.00
Lebanon	2009	34.38	34.38
Liechtenstein	2005	20.00	20.00
Luxembourg	2004	43.33	43.33
Macedonia, FYR	2008	26.41	23.33
Mali	2007	42.23	38.78
Republic of Moldova	2005	25.00	23.76
Monaco	2008	15.00	12.50
Mongolia	2008	21.33	21.33
New Zealand	2008	41.66	40.98
Niger	2004	29.20	29.20
Nigeria	2007	36.18	25.83
Norway	2005	26.74	24.08
Peru	2001	16.66	15.83
Philippines	2001	16.04	15.89
Poland	2007	38.91	38.91
Portugal	2005	39.11	38.26
Romania	2008	14.97	14.97
Samoa	2006	20.41	20.41
Senegal	2001	31.67	31.67
Serbia	2007	24.89	22.00
Singapore	2001	6.49	5.95
Slovak Republic	2006	29.58	28.00
Solomon Islands	2006	58.00	58.00
Suriname	2005	60.41	56.86
Switzerland	2007	22.16	20.50
Syrian Arab Republic	2007	35.54	34.40
Tajikistan	2005	33.33	33.33
Thailand	2007	12.76	11.88
Tunisia	2009	52.34	52.34
Turkey	2007	30.42	27.27
Uganda	2006	36.97	31.63
United Kingdom	2005	22.76	22.76

Notes: For Belarus, we report the professional composition for the 80 newly elected parliamentarians (out of 110 parliamentarians).
In Dominica, 9 out of 31 members of parliament are directly appointed by the head of state.

Table A.3 Subcategories of public servants in national parliaments

Country	Year	Subcategories
Albania	2001	Teachers (19.29%); armed services, police and military (2.86%)
Algeria	2007	Educational profession (14.40%); scientists and researchers (0.26%); civil service and local authority administration (33.68%); armed services, police and military (0.77%)
Andorra	2005	Educational profession (7.14%); civil servants (10.71%)
Argentina	2007	Educational profession (10.98%); scientists and researchers (4.31%); civil servants and administrators (including social and development workers) (1.57%)
Armenia	2007	Educational profession (3.05%); scientists and researchers (12.98%); armed services, police and military (1.53%)
Australia	2004	Lecturers and professors (2.67%); researchers, research assistants, electoral and project officers (7.33%); civil servants and administrators (including social and development workers) (0.67%); public service (5.33%); other administrative officials and administrators (2%)
Austria	2008	Educational profession (10.93%); civil service and local authority administration (7.10%); social workers (0.55%); armed services, police and military (6.01%); international civil servants (2.73%); clerical, secretarial and administration (6.56%)
Azerbaijan	2005	Educational profession (5.22%); scientists and researchers (13.91%); civil servants and administrators (including social and development workers) (6.09%); armed services, police and military (1.74%)
Belarus	2004	Educational profession (27.27%)
Belgium	2007	Educational profession (14.00%); civil servants and administrators (including social and development workers) (10%)
Bosnia and Herzegovina	2002	Professors (4.76%); armed services, police and military (2.38%), sociologists (2.38%)
Bulgaria	2005	Educational profession (7.70%); scientists and researchers (10.38%)
Burkina Faso	2002	Civil servants (45.05%)

– continued on next page –

Table A.3 – continued

Burundi	2005	Educational profession (23.73%); scientists and researchers (4.24%); civil servants and administrators (including social and development workers) (18.64%); armed services, police and military (1.70%)
Central African Republic	2005	Education profession (20.95%); scientists and researchers (4.76%); civil servants and administrators (including social and development workers) (18.10%)
Chile	2009	Educational profession (10.83%); scientists and researchers (7.50%); civil service and local authority administration (1.67%); social workers (0.83%)
Congo, Rep.	2007	Educational profession (21.90%); armed services, police and military (0.73%)
Cyprus	2006	Educational profession (3.57%); scientists and researchers (7.14%); civil servants and administrators (including social and development workers) (10.71%)
Denmark	2007	Educational profession (10.06%); civil servants and administrators (including social and development workers) (35.20%); armed services, police and military (3.91%)
Djibouti	2008	Educational profession (6.15%); civil service and local authority administration (63.08%); armed services, police and military (4.62%)
Dominica	2005	Educational profession (12.90%); civil servants and administrators (including social and development workers) (6.45%); armed services, police and military (6.45%)
Egypt	2007	Educational profession (14.95%); researchers, research assistants, electoral and project officers (0.62%); civil servants (5.30%); armed services, police and military (3.74%)
Estonia	2007	Educational profession (7.92%); scientists and researchers (25.74%); civil servants and administrators (including social and development workers) (5.94%)
France	2007	Educational profession (14.21%); civil servants and administrators (including social and development workers) (15.42%)
Gambia	2002	Teacher (24.53%); civil servants (11.32%); social workers (9.43%); sociologists (1.89%)

– continued on next page –

Table A.3 – continued

Greece	2007	Educational profession (11.33%); scientists and researchers (3.67%); civil servants and administrators (including social and development workers) (3%); armed services, police and military (0.67%)
Haiti	2006	Educational profession (21.43%); scientists and researchers (3.06%); civil servants and administrators (including social and development workers) (2.04%); armed services, police and military (1.02%)
Hungary	2006	Educational profession (17.36%); scientists and researchers (2.85%); civil servants and administrators (including social and development workers) (4.92%); armed services, police and military (0.26%)
Indonesia	2004	Civil servants (4.73%); service and military (4.55%)
Israel	2009	Educational profession (12.50%); scientists and researchers (1.67%); civil servants (1.67%); social workers (0.83%); armed services, police and military (2.5%)
Kuwait	2006	Educational profession (1.54%); scientists and researchers (21.54%); civil servants and administrators (including social and development workers) (12.31%); armed services, police and military (4.62%)
Latvia	2006	Educational profession (11%); scientists and researchers (5%); civil servants, and administrators (including social and development workers) (29%)
Lebanon	2009	Educational profession (30.47%); military and police officers (3.91%)
Liechtenstein	2005	Civil servants (16%); historians (4%)
Luxembourg	2004	Civil servants (36.67%); employees of CFL (Railroad of Luxembourg) (6.67%)
Macedonia, FYR	2008	Educational profession (22.50%); armed services, police and military (0.83%)
Mali	2007	Educational profession (21.09%); scientists and researchers (0.68%); civil servants, and administrators (including social and development workers) (17%)
Moldova	2005	Educational profession (13.86%); scientists and researchers (9.90%)
Monaco	2008	Educational profession (4.17%); civil service and local authority administration (8.33%)

– continued on next page –

Mongolia	2008	Educational profession (9.33%); scientists and researchers (9.33%); civil service and local authority administration (1.33%); armed services, police and military (1.33%)
New Zealand	2008	Educational profession (13.93%); scientists and researchers (2.46%); civil service and local authority administration (18.85%); social workers (1.64%), international civil servants (4.10%)
Niger	2004	Civil servant (29.20%)
Nigeria	2007	Educational profession (10.83%); scientists and researchers (6.39%); civil servants and administrators (including social and development workers) (8.61%)
Norway	2005	Schools, teaching, churches and culture (17.28%); civil servant (6.81%)
Peru	2001	Teacher (5.83%); professors (7.50%); armed services, police and military (0.83%); sociologists (1.67%)
Philippines	2001	Professors (3.27%); civil servants (9.81%); social workers (0.93%); armed services, police and military (1.87%)
Poland	2007	Educational profession (14.13%); scientists and researchers (9.57%); other administrative officials (15.22%)
Portugal	2005	Educational profession (27.83%); scientists and researchers (2.17%); civil servants and administrators (including social and development workers) (7.83%); armed services, police and military (0.43%)
Romania	2008	Educational profession (10.48%); scientists and researchers (2.40%); Civil service and local authority administration (0.90%); armed services, police and military (1.20%)
Senegal	2001	Teacher (25%); civil servants (5.83%); armed services, police and military (0.83%)
Singapore	2001	Professors (5.95%)
Slovak Republic	2006	Educational profession (9.33%); scientists and researchers (9.33%); civil servants and administrators (including social and development workers) (9.33%)
Solomon Islands	2006	Educational profession (14%); civil servants and administrators (including social and development workers) (42%); armed services, police and military (2%)
Suriname	2005	Educational profession (25.49%); scientists and researchers (7.84%); civil servants and administrators (including social and development workers) (23.53%)

– continued on next page –

Table A.3 – continued

Switzerland	2007	Educational profession (8%); scientists and researchers (1.50%); civil servants and administrators (including social and development workers) (9.50%); armed services, police and military (1.50%)
Syrian Arab Republic	2007	Educational profession (14.40%); civil servants and administrators (including social and development workers) (18.00%); armed services, police and military (2%)
Tajikistan	2005	Educational profession (33.33%)
Thailand	2007	Educational profession (1.46%); civil servants and administrators (including social and development workers) (10.42%)
Tunisia	2009	Educational profession (30.84%); civil service and local authority administration (21.50%)
Turkey	2007	Educational profession (22%); scientists and researchers (1.09%); civil servants and administrators (including social and development workers) (3.27%); armed services, police and military (0.91%)
Uganda	2006	Educational profession (13.55%); scientists and researchers (4.22%); civil servants and administrators (including social and development workers) (13.86%); armed services, police and military (3.01%)
Samoa	2006	Educational profession (6.12%); civil servants and administrators (including social and development workers) (14.29%)
Serbia	2007	Educational profession (12%); scientists and researchers (7.60%); civil servants and administrators (including social and development workers) (2.40%)

Notes: The fraction of public servants in the remaining countries were calculated based on the national parliamentary occupational statistics.
Data source: Inter-Parliamentary Union.

Table A.4 Incompatibility regimes in nations in 2010

Country	Regime	Source
Albania	Compatibility	Inter-Parliamentary Union
Algeria	Soft incompatibility	Inter-Parliamentary Union
Andorra	Strict incompatibility	Inter-Parliamentary Union
Argentina	Strict incompatibility	Inter-Parliamentary Union
Armenia	Soft incompatibility	Inter-Parliamentary Union
Australia	Strict incompatibility	Inter-Parliamentary Union
Austria	Soft incompatibility	Austrian Constitution Article 59
Azerbaijan	Strict incompatibility	Inter-Parliamentary Union
Belarus	Soft incompatibility	Inter-Parliamentary Union
Belgium	Strict incompatibility	Inter-Parliamentary Union
Bosnia and Herzegovina	Soft incompatibility	Inter-Parliamentary Union
Bulgaria	Strict incompatibility	Inter-Parliamentary Union
Burkina Faso	Strict incompatibility	Inter-Parliamentary Union
Burundi	Strict incompatibility	Inter-Parliamentary Union
Canada	Soft incompatibility	Inter-Parliamentary Union
Central African Republic	Soft incompatibility	Inter-Parliamentary Union
Chile	Soft incompatibility	Inter-Parliamentary Union
Congo, Rep.	Soft incompatibility	Inter-Parliamentary Union
Cyprus	Strict incompatibility	Inter-Parliamentary Union
Denmark	Compatibility	Inter-Parliamentary Union
Djibouti	Soft incompatibility	Inter-Parliamentary Union
Dominica	Compatibility	Inter-Parliamentary Union
Egypt, Arab Republic	Strict incompatibility	Inter-Parliamentary Union
Estonia	Strict incompatibility	Inter-Parliamentary Union
Finland	Soft incompatibility	Inter-Parliamentary Union
France	Strict incompatibility	Inter-Parliamentary Union
Gambia	Soft incompatibility	Inter-Parliamentary Union
Germany	Strict incompatibility	German Constitution Article 137 and the Law for the members of the German parliament
Greece	Ineligibility	Hellenic Constitution Articles 55-57
Haiti	Ineligibility	Inter-Parliamentary Union
Hungary	Soft incompatibility	Inter-Parliamentary Union
Indonesia	Strict incompatibility	Inter-Parliamentary Union
Ireland	Strict incompatibility	Inter-Parliamentary Union
Israel	Soft incompatibility	Inter-Parliamentary Union
Italy	Strict incompatibility	Inter-Parliamentary Union

– continued on next page –

Table A.4 – continued

Kuwait	Soft incompatibility	Inter-Parliamentary Union
Latvia	Soft incompatibility	Inter-Parliamentary Union
Lebanon	Soft incompatibility	Inter-Parliamentary Union
Liechtenstein	Soft incompatibility	Inter-Parliamentary Union
Luxembourg	Strict incompatibility	Inter-Parliamentary Union
Macedonia, FYR	Strict incompatibility	Inter-Parliamentary Union
Mali	Soft incompatibility	Inter-Parliamentary Union
Moldova	Strict incompatibility	Inter-Parliamentary Union
Monaco	Soft incompatibility	Inter-Parliamentary Union
Mongolia	Strict incompatibility	Inter-Parliamentary Union
Netherlands	Compatibility	Inter-Parliamentary Union
New Zealand	Strict incompatibility	Inter-Parliamentary Union
Niger	Strict incompatibility	Inter-Parliamentary Union
Nigeria	Strict incompatibility	Inter-Parliamentary Union
Norway	Soft incompatibility	Inter-Parliamentary Union
Peru	Strict incompatibility	Inter-Parliamentary Union
Philippines	Strict incompatibility	Inter-Parliamentary Union
Poland	Strict incompatibility	Inter-Parliamentary Union
Portugal	Strict incompatibility	Inter-Parliamentary Union
Romania	Strict incompatibility	Inter-Parliamentary Union
Samoa	Strict incompatibility	Inter-Parliamentary Union
Senegal	Strict incompatibility	Inter-Parliamentary Union
Serbia	Strict incompatibility	Inter-Parliamentary Union
Singapore	Strict incompatibility	Inter-Parliamentary Union
Slovak Republic	Soft incompatibility	Inter-Parliamentary Union
Solomon Islands	Strict incompatibility	Inter-Parliamentary Union
Suriname	Compatibility	Inter-Parliamentary Union
Switzerland	Soft incompatibility	Law for the National Parliament Article 14
Syrian Arab Republic	Strict incompatibility	Inter-Parliamentary Union
Tajikistan	Compatibility	Inter-Parliamentary Union
Thailand	Strict incompatibility	Inter-Parliamentary Union
Tunisia	Strict incompatibility	Inter-Parliamentary Union
Turkey	Strict incompatibility	Inter-Parliamentary Union
Uganda	Ineligibility	Uganda Constitution Articles 77-82
United Kingdom	Ineligibility	House of Commons Disqualification Act
United States	Ineligibility	US Constitution, Article 1, Section 6, Clause 2 and Hatch Act and its amendments

Notes: Some countries apply specific incompatibility rules that complement the general rules considered in the coding which go beyond the public sector.

Persons holding posts for foreign states or for international organizations are incompatible with a parliamentary mandate. This is the case in Burundi, Egypt, Moldova, Niger and Serbia.
Government contractors are incompatible with a parliamentary mandate in Chile, Haiti, Philippines and Thailand.
Australia: Persons with any financial interest in an agreement with the government are declared incompatible unless the responsible parliamentary commission declares the position to be compatible.
Austria: Executives of joint stock companies, banking, commercial, transport and industrial private limited companies, provincial credit institutes and mutual insurance companies are incompatible with a parliamentary mandate unless the responsible parliamentary commission declares the position to be compatible.
Belgium: Lawyers continuously receiving mandates from public authorities are incompatible with a parliamentary mandate.
Dominica: Certain government contractors are incompatible with a parliamentary mandate.
France: Further incompatible offices are 1) posts attributed and remunerated by a foreign state or an international organization and with some exceptions 2) managers or directors of firms i) benefitting from state or local government administration subsidies ii) working principally for or under the control of the state iii) entitled to public savings and iv) involved in real estate.
Greece: The ineligibility rule does not apply to university professors. Furthermore, incompatible with a parliamentary mandate are members of a board of directors, general managers, their alternates, or employees of commercial companies or enterprises enjoying special privileges or subsidies by the state.
Netherlands: Employees of the national parliament as well as public servants of the national public audit institution face an incompatibility rule.
Portugal: Persons holding posts for foreign states or international organizations as well as members of the board of directors of companies in which the state is the majority shareholder are incompatible with a parliamentary mandate.
Senegal: Persons holding posts for international organizations as well as government contractors are incompatible with a parliamentary mandate.
Syrian Arab Republic: Government commissioners and police officers can be elected in another constituency than the one where they are working (after obtaining an authorization).
Tunisia: Persons holding posts for international organizations are incompatible with a parliamentary mandate.
Uganda: Traditional and cultural leaders also face ineligibility.
Unites Kingdom: Educational professions are excluded from the general ineligibility rule applied.

Table A.5 Description of variables

Variable	Description
Control variables	
Ln(GDP per capita)	Natural logarithm of GDP per capita in 2005 converted to international dollars using purchasing power parity rates. *Source: World Development Indicators (World Bank).*
Trade (% of GDP)	Sum of exports and imports of goods and services measured as a share of gross domestic product in 2005. *Source: World Development Indicators (World Bank).*
Employment in services sector (%)	Services sector expressed as a percentage of total employment within the period 2003-2006. The sectors of economic activity are defined according to the International Standard Industrial Classification of All Economic Activities (ISIC), Revision 2 (1968) and Revision 3 (1990). *Source: International Labor Organization.*
Democracy rating	The Freedom House democracy rating summarizes the current state of political rights and civil liberties. On a scale from 1 to 7, a rating of 1 indicates the highest degree of freedom and 7 the lowest level of freedom. We inverted the rating for the year 2000 in order to allow an intuitive interpretation of the results. Moreover, each pair of political rights and civil liberties ratings in 2000 is averaged to determine an overall status of "free", "partly free" or "not free". Countries with averages between 1.0 and 2.5 are considered free, between 3.0 and 5.0 partly free, and between 5.5 and 7.0 not free. *Source: www.freedomhouse.org.*
Disclosure rule index	The variable for disclosure is based on the index of sources publicly available out of the disclosure rule indexes constructed by Djankov et al. (2010). The index measures the ratio of all the source items contained in the country's disclosure form available to the public over all the source items potentially disclosed in the artificial universal form. It measures how many conceivable disclosures of source items are publicly available in practice. The range of the variable is between 0 (no disclosure) and 1 (full disclosure). *Source: Djankov et al. (2010).*

– continued on next page –

Legal origin	Legal origin of the company law or commercial law of each country. Each dummy variable is equal to 1 if the origin of the law of the country is French, German, English, or Scandinavian, respectively, and zero otherwise. *Source: La Porta et al. (2008).*
Majority voting system	The dummy variable for majority voting systems equals 1 if all the members of the lower house are elected under plurality rule, 0 otherwise. *Source: Norris (2009).*
Women in parliament (%)	The fraction of seats in national legislatures going to women in 2005. *Source: Inter-Parliamentary Union.*
Population over 65 years (%)	People aged 65 years and older as a percentage of the total population in 2005. *Source: World Development Indicators (World Bank).*
Population under 15 years (%)	People aged 15 years and younger as a percentage of the total population in 2005. *Source: World Development Indicators (World Bank).*
Ethnic fractionalization	The index of ethnolinguistic fractionalization, approximates the absence of ethnic and linguistic cohesion within a country, ranging from 0 (homogeneous) to 1 (strongly fractionalized) and averaging 5 different indexes. *Source: Alesina et al. (2003).*
Outcome variables	
Government final consumption expenditure (% of GDP)	Average value for the years 2000-2008. General government final consumption expenditure (formerly general government consumption) includes all government current expenditures for purchases of goods and services (including compensation of employees). It also includes most expenditures on national defense and security, but excludes government military expenditures that are part of government capital formation. *Source: World Development Indicators (World Bank).*

– continued on next page –

Table A.5 – continued

Kaufmann corruption index	Average score of the Kaufmann corruption index for the years 2003, 2005 and 2007. Perceived control of corruption captures the extent to which public power is exercised for private gain, including both petty and grand forms of corruption, as well as "capture" of the state by elites and private interests. The index is one of the composite measures of governance generated by the UCM. It is in units of a standard normal distribution with mean zero, a standard deviation of one, and running from approximately -2.5 to 2.5, with higher values corresponding to better governance; i.e., less corruption. *Source: Kaufmann et al. (2008).*

Table A.6
Robustness analysis for alternative institutional and economic determinants of political selection
Sample: "At least partly free democracies"; Dependent variable: Adjusted fraction of public servants (%)

	I	II	III	IV	V	VI
Strict incompatibility or ineligibility	–7.449**	–6.871*	–6.900*	–7.192*	–6.883*	–7.220**
	(3.59)	(3.52)	(3.83)	(4.10)	(3.78)	(3.37)
Ln(GDP per capita)	–1.605	–1.458	–0.805	–1.116	–1.632	–3.024
	(1.47)	(1.43)	(1.54)	(1.64)	(1.53)	(2.52)
Democracy rating	0.670	1.114	1.944	0.612	0.425	2.266
	(1.88)	(1.85)	(2.13)	(2.04)	(2.13)	(1.74)
Majority voting system		7.777*				
		(4.04)				
Disclosure rule index			–10.901			
			(7.47)			
UK legal origin				–1.810		
				(4.91)		
German legal origin				–3.115		
				(5.26)		
Scandinavian legal origin				8.167		
				(9.47)		
Fraction of women in parliament					0.112	
					(0.24)	
Fraction of employment in services sector						0.398
						(0.25)
No. of obs.	59	59	54	55	57	47
R^2	.088	.146	.123	.119	.077	.235
Prob. $> F$	0.166	0.069	0.163	0.390	0.374	0.022

Notes: OLS estimations. Standard errors in parentheses. The dependent variable is adjusted for the category "unknown professions" in national statistics. The reference category in panel II is a proportional or a mixed-member electoral system. In panel IV, the reference category is French legal origin. Significance levels: * $.05 < p < .1$, ** $.01 < p < .05$, *** $p < .01$.

Appendix B

Data on public servants in German Laender parliaments

Information on the occupational background of the members of the German Laender parliaments is mainly collected from entries in the parliamentary handbooks. Entries for single members were coded and summed to determine the fraction of public servants in parliament. If available, summary statistics from parliamentary handbooks or other sources were considered. Table B.1 provides a detailed account of the sources by legislative period (LP).

Table B.1
Data sources for the fraction of public servants in German Laender parliaments

Baden-Württemberg
LP 1-6: Occupational statistics from parliamentary handbooks.
LP 7-14: Occupational statistics from parliamentary handbooks, corrected for the category members and former members of the government based on entries for single members of parliament.

Bavaria
LP 1-6: Occupational statistics from parliamentary handbooks.
LP 7-8: Occupational statistics from parliamentary handbooks, corrected for mayors and district administrators.
LP 9-12: Occupational statistics from parliamentary handbooks, corrected for the category members and former members of the government based on entries for single members of parliament.
LP 13-15: Occupational statistics from parliamentary handbooks.

Berlin
LP 5: Nauber (1970).
LP 6-14: Own coding based on entries in the parliamentary handbooks for single members.
LP 15-16: Own coding based on the parliamentary online database containing individual entries.

Bremen
LP 4-7: Own coding based on entries in the parliamentary handbooks for single members.
LP 8: Hess (1976).
LP 9-16: Occupational statistics from parliamentary handbooks.
LP 17: Own coding based on the parliamentary online database containing individual entries.

Continuation of Table B.1

Hamburg LP 7-18: parliamentary handbooks. LP 19: own coding based on the parliamentary online database containing individual entries.
Hesse LP 1-4: Schrode (1977). LP 5: Holl (1989). LP 6-10: Own coding based on entries in the parliamentary handbook (Lengemann 1987) for single members. LP 11-16: Occupational statistics from parliamentary handbooks. LP 17: Occupational statistics from the parliamentary online database.
Lower Saxony LP 1-15: Occupational statistics from parliamentary handbooks. LP 16: Occupational statistics from the parliamentary online database.
North Rhine-Westphalia LP 2-14: Occupational statistics from parliamentary handbooks.
Rhineland-Palatinate LP 1-3: Own coding based on entries in the parliamentary handbook (Landtag Rheinland-Pfalz 1987) for single members. LP 4-6: Schrode (1977). LP 7-15: Own coding based on entries in the parliamentary handbook (Landtag Rheinland-Pfalz 1987) for single members.
Saar LP 1-12: Rütters (2003). LP 13: Own coding based on entries in the parliamentary handbook for single members.
Schleswig-Holstein LP 3-9: Occupational statistics from parliamentary handbooks. LP 10: Own coding based on entries in the parliamentary handbook for single members. LP 11-15: Occupational statistics from parliamentary handbooks. LP 16: Own coding based on the parliamentary online database containing individual entries.
Brandenburg LP 1-3: Lübker and Schüttemeyer (2004). LP 4: Occupational statistics from parliamentary handbooks.
Mecklenburg-Lower-Pomerania LP 2-5: Own coding based on entries in the parliamentary handbook for single members.

Continuation of Table B.1

Saxony LP 1-2: Patzelt (1997). LP 3-5: Own coding based on entries in the parliamentary handbook for single members.
Saxony-Anhalt LP 1-5: Own coding based on entries in the parliamentary handbook for single members.
Thuringia LP 1-4: Thüringer Landtag (2005).

Table B.2
Descriptive statistics for the fraction of public servants elected to German Laender parliaments

	No. of LPs	Mean	Std. dev.	Min.	Max.
Old Laender					
Baden-Württemberg	14	47.39	9.10	29.00	61.60
Bavaria	15	40.45	9.91	23.80	53.43
Berlin	12	39.91	6.95	25.00	48.85
Bremen	14	38.29	7.35	30.12	55.00
Hamburg	13	33.49	4.93	23.14	41.66
Hesse	17	46.56	7.91	32.50	55.45
Lower Saxony	16	29.28	12.28	10.60	42.58
North Rhine-Westphalia	13	30.24	8.88	15.34	41.50
Rhineland-Palatinate	15	45.26	12.63	24.20	60.00
Saar	13	43.22	11.25	26.00	58.00
Schleswig-Holstein	14	43.34	8.25	24.60	58.10
New Laender					
Brandenburg	4	40.84	7.28	31.50	48.90
Meckl.-Lower-Pomerania	4	38.73	8.64	28.17	46.48
Saxony	4	44.45	6.48	35.48	50.80
Saxony-Anhalt	5	31.04	5.39	24.50	37.73
Thuringia	4	33.20	1.63	31.40	35.20
Sum old Laender	156	39.88	10.98	10.60	61.60
Sum new Laender	21	37.34	7.62	24.50	50.80
Sum all Laender	177	39.58	10.65	10.60	61.60

Note: LPs indicates the number of legislative periods.

Sources: See Table B.1.

Table B.3
Institutions characterizing the legal status of public servants in the German Laender parliaments (part 1)

	Strict incompatibility	Soft incompatibility	Pension benefit	Abeyance compensation
Baden-Württemberg	LP 1 (1952)	as of LP 2 (1956)	LP 5-7 (1968-1980)	as of LP 2 (1956)
Bavaria	as of LP 7 (1970)	never applied	LP 7-8 (1970-1978)	LP 7-8 (1970-1978)
Berlin	never applied	never applied	never applied	never applied
Bremen	as of LP 7 (1967)	never applied	as of LP 10 (1979)	as of LP 7 (1967)
Hamburg	never applied	applies to all observed periods (as of 1970)	never applied	never applied
Hesse	as of LP 8 (1974)	LP 2-7 (1950-1974)	LP 7-8 (1970-1978)	LP 2-8 (1950-1978)
Lower Saxony	as of LP 1 (1947)	never applied	LP 7-8 (1970-1978)	LP 5-8 (1963-1978)
North Rhine-Westphalia	applies to all observed periods (as of 1950)	never applied	LP 6-8 (1966-1980)	LP 3-8 (1958-1980)
Rhineland-Palatinate	as of LP 8 (1975)	LP 2-7 (1951-1971)	LP 7-8 (1971-1979)	LP 2-11 (1951-1991)
Saar	LP 2-3 (1952-1959) and as of LP 7 (1975)	LP 1 (1947) and LP 4-6 (1960-1975)	LP 6-7 (1970-1980)	LP 2-10 (1952-1994)
Schleswig-Holstein	LP 8 (1975) and (re)introduction in 2006, which applies to election in 2010	LP 3-7 (1954-1975) and LP 9-16 (1979-2010)	LP 7-8 (1971-1979)	LP 4-12 (1958-1992)
Brandenburg	as of LP 1 (1990)	never applied	never applied	never applied

Continuation of Table B.3

Mecklenburg-Lower-Pomerania	never applied	as of LP 1 (1990)	never applied	never applied
Saxony	never applied	as of LP 1 (1990)	never applied	never applied
Saxony-Anhalt	as of LP 1 (1990)	never applied	never applied	never applied
Thuringia	as of LP 1 (1990)	never applied	never applied	never applied

Notes: Listed are the legislative periods (LP) for which the specific rules were in force from the beginning of the terms.

Hesse: For the 1st legislative period (1946), we assume that there was no incompatibility rule in force because the first law concerning incompatibility was enacted in 1948 (GVBl. p. 101). Moreover, Mallmann (1953) notes the tendency towards compatibility in the newly formed Laender (except the Laender initially governed by the occupying power United Kingdom (UK)).

Lower Saxony: The 1st legislative period (1947) is coded as strict incompatibility although the occupying power (UK) introduced an ineligibility rule, enacted in the first state election law. No separate variable for this stricter regulation is defined because it is unclear whether there was not still an implicit reemployment guarantee.

North Rhine-Westphalia: The 2nd legislative period (beginning in 1950), we coded as strict incompatibility although the occupying powers (UK) introduced an ineligibility rule, enacted in the first (1947) as well as in the second state election law in 1950 (GVBl. No. 13 p. 45). As it is unclear whether there was not still a reemployment guarantee, no separate variable is defined. The first law on the legal status of public servants elected to parliament in 1954 (GV. NW. p. 147) imposed an incompatibility rule for all public servants except teachers and university professors. This exception was in force until 1978. As teachers and university professors were the only exceptions, we coded a strict incompatibility.

Rhineland-Palatinate: For two reasons, we assume that there was no incompatibility rule in force for the 1st legislative period (1946). First, Kriegbaum (1967) refers to Article 95 of the first constitution (1947) of Rhineland-Palatinate which declares no need for a leave of absence while exercising a political mandate (VOBl. No. 14). Second, Eschenburg (1952) and Mallmann (1953) describe the tendency towards compatibility in the newly formed Laender. With regard to pension benefits, the law on the remuneration of members of parliaments, introduced in 1960, comprised an optional old-age pension. However, a binding old-age pension scheme was introduced only in 1969. The variable indicating twice accounted years for pension entitlements was consequently coded as 1 beginning with the 7th legislative period in 1971.

Saar: For the 1st legislative period (1947), a soft incompatibility rule is assumed for three reasons. First, the electoral law, introduced in 1952, comprised a soft incompatibility rule. Second, in the first state constitution (1947), no explicit incompatibility principles were laid down. Third, the occupying power France itself preferred some kind of soft incompatibility rule (Schmidt 1970: 188).

Table B.3
Institutions characterizing the legal status of public servants in the German Laender parliaments (part 2)

	Full-time parliament	Automatic promotion	Other privileges
Baden-Württemberg	never applied; introduction in 2011	never applied	LP 2-7 (1956-1980)
Bavaria	as of LP 9 (1978)	LP 7-8 (1970-1978)	LP 7-8 (1970-1978)
Berlin	never applied	never applied	never applied
Bremen	never applied	LP 7-9 (1967-1979)	LP 7-9 (1967-1979)
Hamburg	never applied	never applied	LP 7-8 (1970-1978)
Hesse	as of LP 9 (1978)	never applied	LP 2-8 (1950-1978)
Lower Saxony	as of LP 9 (1978)	never applied	LP 5-8 (1963-1978)
North Rhine-Westphalia	as of LP 9 (1980)	never applied	LP 3-8 (1954-1980)
Rhineland-Palatinate	as of LP 12 (1991)	never applied	LP 2-8 (1951-1979)
Saar	as of LP 8 (1980)	never applied	LP 2-7 (1952-1980)
Schleswig-Holstein	as of LP 8 (1979)	never applied	LP 4-8 (1958-1979)
Brandenburg	as of LP 1 (1990)	never applied	never applied
Mecklenburg-Lower-Pomerania	as of LP 1 (1990)	never applied	never applied
Saxony	as of LP 1 (1990)	never applied	never applied
Saxony-Anhalt	as of LP 1 (1990)	never applied	never applied
Thuringia	as of LP 1 (1990)	never applied	never applied

Table B.4
Descriptive statistics for the prevalence of the different institutions

	Mean
Strict incompatibility	51.41
Soft incompatibility	42.37
Pension benefit	14.69
Abeyance compenstion	40.11
Full-time parliament	38.98
Automatic promotion	2.82
Other privileges	27.12
Strict incompatibility x full-time parliament	29.94
Soft incompatibility x full-time parliament	9.04

Appendix C

Box C.1 Control instruments in German Laender parliaments

Major interpellation

Major interpellations (often called *grosse Anfrage* or *Interpellation*) are addressed to the government, are submitted in the form of a detailed written request to the president of the parliament, and have to be signed by a parliamentary group or by a minimum of five to fifteen legislators. In some Laender parliaments, one parliamentarian is the main supporter of the submission. The government is requested to provide a written reply within six weeks. After a reply is received, the interpellation is placed on the plenary agenda, and if the submitting group insists, a debate must take place. Prior to a debate, one of the questioners is allowed to present additional arguments backing the submitted interpellation. After the debate, parliamentarians can induce a motion for a resolution to express their opinion on the subject of the interpellation or the government's reply to it.

Minor interpellation

Minor interpellations (often called *kleine* or *schriftliche Anfrage*) are submitted by individual legislators in the form of a detailed written request containing up to ten specific questions. The government is expected to reply to the minor interpellation, in writing, within two weeks. The answer is published as parliamentary printed matter. If a minor interpellation is not answered in time, rules of procedure stipulate a transformation into a major interpellation.

Oral inquiry

They are also submitted by individual legislators in the form of a written request containing up to five specific questions. They must be sent some days before the next plenary debate takes place (previous notice). Their authors read them out and the government has to give an oral answer. Follow-up questions are allowed. The author is asked to express his or her (dis)satisfaction with the answer provided. If oral questions are not answered, the government has to deliver a written reply; otherwise, it is put forward to a minor interpellation.

Box C.2 Example of a minor interpellation

The example of a minor interpellation is taken from the 4th legislative period of the parliament of Mecklenburg-Lower-Pomerania. It was executed on November 26, 2003 (parliamentary printed matter 4/919). The interpellation was submitted by Harry Glawe, a member of parliament with a public service background.

Topic: Status of employee ill-health in the ministerial administration of Mecklenburg-Lower-Pomerania

(a) *The government ministries of Mecklenburg-Lower-Pomerania conduct a very different policy regarding the reporting of employee ill-health statistics. Are there particular reasons?*

(b) *Do flexible vacation days influence the time structure of employee ill-health absences? Are the absences recorded, and if so, how detailed are the records?*

(c) *How many members of staff are ill for more than six weeks (give as a percentage also)? Please give detailed information for each ministry. How has the number of absences of more than six weeks owing to ill-health developed over the past five years?*

(d) *What is the annual average number of ill staff? What is the ratio of annually ill staff to annual working hours?*

(e) *What criteria does the government apply in appraising the average level of staff ill in relation to the annual working hours?*

(f) *What criteria does the government apply in appraising a comparison between the different ill-health statistics of the individual ministries?*

(g) *How do these figures compare with parallel government institutions in other German regions?*

Note: The example is not translated literally but with regard to content.
Sources: Parliamentary online documentation services.

Table C.1
Descriptive statistics for the dependent and independent variables

	N of LP	Mean	Std. dev.	Min.	Max.
Dependent variables					
Major interpellations	152	66.583	53.56	0	237
Minor interpellations	153	1663.634	1723.853	7	12278
Oral inquiries	133	545.871	546.931	3	2499
Independent variables					
Fraction of public servants	153	40.481	10.363	10.6	61.6
Mixed-member electoral system	153	.739	.441	0	1
Margin of victory	153	11.799	8.858	.1	41.5
New party	153	.333	.473	0	1
Number of parties	153	3.706	.924	2	8
Seat share of the SPD	153	40.794	9.806	10.484	62.162
Coalition government by major parties	153	.144	.352	0	1
Constitutional parliament	153	.059	.236	0	1
Oral inquiries exercised	153	.346	.477	0	1
LP shorter than 1.5 years	153	.033	.178	0	1
LP lasting between 1.5 and 3 years	153	.039	.195	0	1
LP lasting regular 4 years	153	.686	.466	0	1
LP lasting regular 5 years	153	.242	.430	0	1

Note: LP stands for legislative period. The time series of minor interpellations for Hamburg also includes the number of oral inquiries submitted. The Hamburg parliament documentation service does not separately document the use of both instruments. However, the number of minor interpellation dominates the number of oral inquiries submitted.

Sources: For the dependent variables, see Kalke and Raschke (2004), Mielke and Reutter (2004), Raschke and Kalke (1994), Reutter (2008), Schäfer (2005), and various parliamentary handbooks and parliamentary documentation systems.

For the independent variables, see B.1 and B.2 in the Appendix for the fraction of public servants, Massicotte (2003) for the coding of the variable electoral system, and Manow and Wettengel (2006) for the coding of the form of government. For all other variables, the coding is based on information from the *Bundes-* or *Landeswahlleiter*.

Appendix D

Figure D.1
Development of aggregate senior official employment in the ministerial bureaucracy of Schleswig-Holstein.

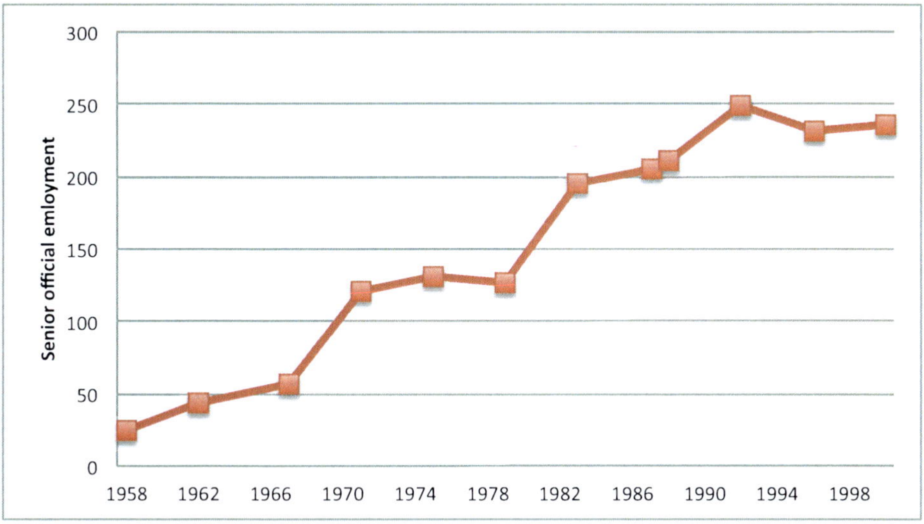

Notes: The aggregate development of senior official employment is adjusted to entire legislative periods. In 2000, 4,807 senior officials are counted in the ministerial bureaucracies of the ten German Laender. The respective number in 1960 is 524.
Sources: See Table D.1.

Table D.1 Descriptive statistics for the dependent and independent variables

	N of LP	Mean	Std. dev.	Min.	Max.
Dependent variable					
Percentage change in the senior official employment	116	28.419	49.672	-16.227	251.111
Independent variables					
Government led by the SPD	116	0.431	0.497	0	1
Major change in the composition of government	116	0.103	0.306	0	1
Minor change in the composition of government	116	0.267	0.444	0	1
Percentage-point change in the fraction of public servants in parliament	114	1.19	6.07	–15.19	21
Independent variables for additional robustness checks					
Reform period (1966-1973)	116	0.164	0.372	0	1
Percentage change in population	104	1.296	2.604	–3.026	10.862
Percentage change in per capita income	85	7.443	5.806	–5.79	18.45
Percentage-point change in the unemployment rate	101	0.901	2.293	–4.90	8.20
Fraction of public servants in parliament	116	43.094	9.977	14.09	61.60

Note: The dependent variable is adjusted for the length of the legislative period.
Sources: The dependent variable is taken from Manow and Wettengel (2006) and adjusted for legislative periods.
For the independent variables, see Tables B.1 and B.2 in the Appendix for the representation of public servants in parliament, Manow and Wettengel (2006) for the political partisanship of government, and the major and minor changes in the composition of (coalition) governments. These variables are complemented with information provided by the German electoral commission (*Bundeswahlleiter*). The percentage change in population, in per capita income as well as the change in the unemployment rate are taken from the German statistical office (*Statistisches Bundesamt*). These latter variables are adjusted for entire legislative periods.